Frontiers in Market Access

A Practical Approach to Mastering Market Access in Emerging Markets

KASEM S. AKHRAS

Frontiers in Market Access
Copyright © 2021 Kasem S. Akhras
First published in 2021

Print: 978-1-922456-32-8
E-book: 978-1-922456-33-5
Hardback: 978-1-922456-34-2

All rights reserved. No part of this book may be reproduced, stored in a retrieval system, or transmitted by any means (electronic, mechanical, photocopying, recording, or otherwise) without written permission from the author.

Because of the dynamic nature of the Internet, any web addresses or links contained in this book may have changed since publication and may no longer be valid. The information in this book is based on the author's experiences and opinions. The views expressed in this book are solely those of the author and do not necessarily reflect the views of the publisher; the publisher hereby disclaims any responsibility for them.

The author of this book does not dispense any form of medical, legal, financial, or technical advice either directly or indirectly. Opinions expressed in this book are mine and do not represent my current or previous employers. The intent of the author is solely to provide information of a general nature to help you in your quest for personal development and growth. In the event you use any of the information in this book, the author and the publisher assume no responsibility for your actions. If any form of expert assistance is required, the services of a competent professional should be sought.

Publishing information
Publishing, design, and production facilitated by Passionpreneur Publishing, A division of Passionpreneur Organization Pty Ltd
ABN: 48640637529

www.PassionpreneurPublishing.com
Melbourne, VIC | Australia

To my parents, Saleh and Ratiba. My father inspired me to lead by example and take the high road in everything I did. And my mother taught me at a young age how to be brave and always aim high.

CONTENTS

List of Tables and Figures	7
List of Abbreviations	9
Acknowledgments	11
Introduction *Transforming the Market Access Function*	13
Chapter 1 *The Health-Care and Pharmaceutical Market*	21
Chapter 2 *The Winning Market Access Mindset*	33
Chapter 3 *Pricing and Market Access*	45
Chapter 4 *Value and Market Access*	61
Chapter 5 *Delivering Winning Market Access Solutions*	75
Chapter 6 *New Evolving Access Models*	89
Chapter 7 *The Winning Market Access Team*	101
Chapter 8 *Negotiations to Win Access*	109
Conclusion *Three Takeaways*	115
About the Author	117

LIST OF TABLES AND FIGURES

Table 1: MENA region key indicators — 23

Table 2: Economic and health indicators for MENA countries — 24

Table 3: Challenges facing the pharmaceutical industry in the MENA region — 29

Figure 1: MENA health expenditures in contrast to other countries — 25

Figure 2: Strategic approach to market access throughout product life cycle — 34

Figure 3: Coordinated approach to market access — 36

Figure 4: Impact of market access planning and execution on product launch — 39

Figure 5: The five key pillars of successful market access strategy — 41

Figure 6: Approach to stakeholders engagement on value creation — 43

Figure 7: Reference countries used in IRP in MENA countries — 48

Figure 8: Factors used in value-based pricing of innovative pharmaceutical products — 50

Figure 9: Factors that impact the value perception of products — 53

Figure 10: Impact of launch sequence on price setting — example — 55

Figure 11: The evolving health-care ecosystem — the old and the new — 63

Figure 12: The pharmaceutical budget in perspective — 65

Figure 13: Definition of value in health-care — 66

Figure 14: Approach to policy shaping activities to promote value-based care 73

Figure 15: Patient access schemes 78

Figure 16: Approach to stakeholders mapping for market access 86

Figure 17: Summary of product access strategy by account/customer 88

Figure 18: Affordability pyramid and goal of market access 90

Figure 19: Types of patient affordability programs 93

Figure 20: Patient affordability programs design elements 95

LIST OF ABBREVIATIONS

AB	Access Brand
CAGR	Compound Annual Growth Rate
COO	Country of Origin
CIF	Cost, Insurance, and Freight
EM	Emerging Market
EMR	Electronic Medical Records
FOB	Freight on Board
FOC	Free of Charge
GDP	Gross Domestic Product
GPT	Global Project Team
HEOR	Health Economics and Outcomes Research
HrQOL	Health-Related Quality of Life
HTA	Health Technology Assessment
IP	Intellectual Property
IRP	International Reference Pricing
IQVIA	Data science and technology company formed in 2016 from the merger of Quintiles and IMS Health
KAM	Key Account Management
KPI	Key Performance Indicators
KVM	Key Value Messages

MA	Market Access
MAH	Market Authorization Holder
MEA	Managed Entry Agreements
MENA	Middle East and North Africa region
MNC	Multinational Company
MOH	Ministry of Health
OBA	Outcomes-Based Agreements
OOP	Out-of-Pocket Costs
PAP	Patient Affordability Program
P&L	Profit and Loss
PPP	Purchasing Power Parity
RDP	Regulatory Data Protection
RSA	Risk-Share Agreement
RWD	Real-World Data
RWE	Real-World Evidence
TPC	Third-Party Company
VBC	Value-Based Care
VBP	Value-Based Pricing
WB	World Bank
WTP	Willingness to Pay

ACKNOWLEDGMENTS

The publication of this book would not have been possible without the blessing of Allah, Almighty God (SWT).[1]

In the spirit of the saying "he who does not thank people will not thank Allah," I would like to sincerely acknowledge and thank the many friends and colleagues who encouraged me to write a book on this topic. I would also like to extend my heartfelt gratitude to my early mentor and advisor Hind T. Hatoum, Ph.D. for her encouragement to pursue pharmacoeconomics and outcomes research as a career. Special thanks also to Peter Lauper, Ph.D., Gilbert Verkuijlen, M.Sc., and Omar Dabbous, M.D. for their trust and continued support.

This undertaking, and my qualifications to write this book, also would not have happened without the unwavering support and inspiration of my wife and children, who put up with my long working hours, often even on weekends, and my hectic travel schedule. Thank you with all my love.

---

1 SWT in Arabic stands for *Subhanahu wa ta'ala*, which translates as "Glory to Him, the Exalted" or "Glorious and Exalted Is He."

INTRODUCTION

TRANSFORMING THE MARKET ACCESS FUNCTION

Where there's a will there's a way

This may be an old saying but it is a wise one, and a principle that I live by, both in my personal and professional life.

After spending 17 years in the pharmaceutical industry in the United States as a global leader in health economics and outcomes research (HEOR), managed markets, and market access (MA), focusing on developed pharmaceutical markets, I moved to emerging markets (EMs) in the Middle East and North Africa (MENA) region, where the markets are very different, to lead the MA function. The three challenges I faced after my move were the technical capability of the people working in the field, the mindset, and the overall health-care environment and market dynamics.

From the technical-capability standpoint, I found that the organizations and people knew the importance of MA as a critical function for the future growth and success of an organization; however, the core capabilities needed (pricing, HEOR, economic modeling, real-world evidence, etc.) for MA were lacking both internally (within the companies) and externally from the payer's side (private and public). The mindset of the people was also different.

Generally, professionals were very interested in market access and the new ways things were done in this field in other parts of the world, but the interest did not always translate into driving these new trends in their daily practice—partly because of their limited capabilities but also because of the overall environment in the MENA region.

In the health-care environment and market dynamics, the biggest challenge was the volatility coming from several areas—the pharmaceutical-pricing environment, abrupt decision-making with rapid implementation, and the lack of transparency and predictability in decision-making.

However, armed with global experience in dealing with several international markets across different therapeutic areas, a good understanding of people's mindsets and behaviors and how to deal with them, and my strong belief in the importance of "the will" to show people how they could be successful in implementing new ideas, I was able to establish myself as an expert in the area even though I was new to this part of the world. As time went by, I tried several strategies to address the situation. I would share relevant articles so people could read and learn from them and share case studies as an example of "how" it was done. I also approached academic institutions to try to set up joint fellowship programs in HEOR and MA to enhance capabilities. However, as HEOR and MA were new to the region, locals did not have a basic background in the key skill sets needed, and so they were more receptive to sitting down and listening or taking part in workshops and interacting with people rather than reading articles. They were more interested in reading "how to do things" so they could move into implementation. I also noticed that many of the general managers and area vice presidents who came to the region on international assignments did not necessarily have good background knowledge of the health-care and pharmaceutical markets of the MENA region. And because of their short-term assignments (usually two to four years), long-term investment and proper funding in building HEOR and MA teams, although recognized as a critical need, was always tough to achieve.

Through giving many presentations, holding training workshops, and taking part in panel discussions internally, within the companies, and externally, at regional conferences, I had countless encounters with people who told me how they appreciated my expertise and the way I approached the issues and proposed solutions. So I put my expertise to use to help the professionals in the industry and eventually help management executives develop a better understanding of the MA environment in the region. Below are some of my key achievements and qualifications over my 24 years in the pharmaceutical industry:

- Established market access, government affairs and policy, pricing, and tender functions for top multinational companies (MNCs).
- Led the Pharmaceutical Industry Working Group in MENA on pricing, value, and access; represented the industry in discussions with regulatory authorities on policy issues; and led major studies commissioned by the industry to measure the footprint, value, and impact of the industry on key socio-economic indicators in countries where the industry operates in the region.
- Invited to speak at key regional conferences about market access and health policy.
- Authored more than 45 peer-reviewed journal articles and presented more than 70 papers and/or podium presentations at regional and international medical conferences.
- Mentored many MA professional staff who went on to take leading positions in market access with major MNCs.
- Established guidance and standard operating procedures that govern how to design and implement MA solutions sustainably.
- Launched many innovative pharmaceutical products with different access solutions to secure optimal pricing, reimbursement, and formulary listings.
- Designed and implemented different types of patient-access solutions to overcome affordability challenges for several high-value products.
- Conducted several workshops with key formulary and reimbursement decision-makers in the private and public sectors on key topics related to pharmaceutical pricing, cost-effectiveness studies, tender management, and managing pharmaceutical budgets as part of cost-containment measures.

Having done all of this—motivated by my passion for patient access and my strong belief that passing on one's knowledge to others is a duty—I realized the need for this book.

I am passionate about health-care and even more passionate about improving patient access to health-care in general and pharmaceutical care in particular. This has made me want to share my 24 years of experience with the professionals who want to make a career in market access, health policy, and/or government affairs.

I have also been inspired to write this book by the many colleagues who have asked me for recommendations on "a book that they can read on MA." Many have even suggested that I write a book on the subject. This is when I started thinking about producing a practical book for EM professionals and those who want to enter the pharmaceutical market with a career in market access, a book that would also be valuable to senior management coming to the region or those who are interested in developing a better understanding of the MENA region.

Now, I am sharing my knowledge in the form of this book to help:

- MA professionals working in the biopharmaceutical industry, especially those who are working in emerging markets
- government affairs and policy professionals who want to understand MA essentials as part of their effort to shape the health-care ecosystem
- health-professional students (medical, pharmacy, public health)
- pharmaceutical executives who are interested in developing a better understanding of market access as a key success factor for the growth of their company
- global HEOR teams that develop value and access dossiers for new products
- commercial teams (strategic marketing) and global product teams that launch new products globally, including in emerging markets.

I strongly believe that uplifting people's capabilities will be a win-win for everyone—for pharmaceutical companies that are looking for good talent to hire; for young professionals who are entering the field and will become decision-makers; and, most importantly, for the patients in the region. The more market access is understood by all stakeholders in the field, the easier it will be for patients to access pharmaceutical innovations.

So, I hope this book gives you what you are looking for. As you read on, you will learn that all markets have unique challenges from an MA perspective and that the goal of market access is to find an integrated way to work with the system to solve problems and overcome access obstacles.

But before we go into the technical aspects of market access, it is important to understand the big picture—that is, the overall health-care setting that you operate in, whether you work in developed markets, emerging markets, or international markets. Let's start by looking at the big picture.

The big picture

Have you ever asked yourself: Why do some companies struggle to commercialize a product despite it being novel and well-differentiated and able to meet a high unmet medical need? Did they expect the product to sell itself?

The fact is, there are many examples of products with strong value propositions, and the potential to meet high unmet medical needs, that nonetheless do not perform as expected. The reason is that these companies do not have the right MA strategy and organizational mindset to ensure that the product will be a success.

One of the most common misconceptions about market access in growth markets is that you can take people who have done commercial roles—key account management (KAM) could be one example—or people who have done regulatory affairs roles, give them MA responsibility, and expect them to be successful at it. While it is true that having a commercial and/or regulatory affairs background can be helpful, the MA function requires far more important skill sets than just commercial and/or regulatory affairs. Some people even think of market access as being all about pricing, which is far from the truth.

A successful MA career requires specific knowledge in HEOR, pricing, real-world evidence, evidence-based medicine, and health policy, in addition to skills in strategic marketing. It also requires a mindset that drives the behavior of both the individual who has MA responsibility and the cross-functional teams responsible for the product.

The rest of this book is divided into eight chapters that cover the key topics in market access:

1. **The health-care and pharmaceutical market:** This opening chapter discusses the overall health-care environment in the MENA region, using it as an example of a major emerging market for all the major MNCs in the pharmaceutical industry. Here, you will understand the key aspects of health-care financing and market dynamics, which play a key role in access to health-care in general and the pharmaceutical industry in particular.

2. **The winning market access mindset:** Here you will learn more about the winning mindset, the importance of starting MA planning early, and the need to have cross-functional alignment on the five key pillars that MA activities should focus on throughout the product life cycle. We will also discuss what an MA mindset entails and the importance of stakeholder engagement.

3. **Pricing and market access:** This chapter discusses the key pricing principles and mechanisms used in pharmaceutical pricing, reimbursement, and formulary inclusions. We will also talk about the importance of pricing considerations on product launch sequencing and its impact on pricing volatility in the market.

4. **Value and market access:** Here we talk about the importance of focusing on the value and not just the pricing of pharmaceuticals, and why it is vital from an MA perspective to articulate the value to all stakeholders in the ecosystem before discussing the price. We also discuss value-based decision-making and how to shape the evolving ecosystem to shift the focus from price to value.

5. **Delivering winning market access solutions:** This chapter is about practical approaches to developing and implementing MA solutions that address market dynamics and payer challenges.

6. **New evolving market access models:** Given the evolving market dynamics and growing payer challenges, you will learn about the two important trends and evolving business models in access solutions—patient affordability programs (PAP) and

multi-branding—as strategies to overcome the affordability obstacles that are common to many emerging markets.
7. **The winning market access team:** This chapter discusses ways to build excellent MA capabilities and the important organizational considerations in this regard.
8. **Negotiations to win access:** Finally, we will discuss the importance of mastering negotiations to manage market volatility.

By the time you reach the end of the book, you will have a much better understanding of the following key success factors for winning market access in an emerging market:

- Deep knowledge and understanding of the overall socio-economic and political dynamics of the local market environment that we operate in.
- A winning MA mindset that understands stakeholders' challenges and brings about a win-win solution to overcome access barriers.
- An appreciation of price as a reflection of value: the *price* is what patients pay for products, but the *value* is what they get. It's very important that the value is well articulated and appreciated by stakeholders.
- An ability to deliver customizable solutions that are fit-for-purpose to improve access and overcome payer concerns.
- Learning agility and readiness to develop and/or adopt new trends and business models to make patient access to innovative medicine as good as it can be.
- The knowledge that, in the end, winning market access is not all about the commercial success of the pharmaceutical company. It is about creating solutions that expedite patient access to innovative therapy in an emerging market. Failure to do that will result in unfair and inequitable access, which can create several social problems and an unsustainable health-care system.

Now that you have a fair idea of what the book entails and the learnings you can expect from each of the key topics, let's move on to the next chapter, where you will get an insight into the overall health-care environment in the MENA region.

1

THE HEALTH-CARE AND PHARMACEUTICAL MARKET

There has never been a time when timely access to health-care in general and pharmaceuticals, in particular, has been more important than it is now. We see a huge demand for health-care services, driven by the growing population in the MENA region, the constant flow of high-value innovations (not only on the pharmaceutical side but also on the diagnostics and all aspects of the care continuum), and a well-informed public, including patients—thanks to the Internet of Things and the growth of social media.

Consider the following global facts. IQVIA has estimated that global spending on medicine in 2020 was one and a half trillion dollars, an increase of about 29 to 32 percent from 2015, compared to an increase of 35 percent in the prior five years. In 2020, more of the world's population had access to medicine than ever before, albeit with substantial disparities. Patients had greater access to breakthrough therapies and innovations around hepatitis C, a range of cancer medicines, autoimmune diseases, heart diseases, and various other rare diseases, and there was a shift in medicine from mass-marketed products to specialty medicine that came with a high price tag.

From a MENA perspective, let's also consider the following facts supplied by the World Bank (WB). While the world population grew 8 percent in the period 2010–2017, the MENA region grew at 14 to 16 percent. From a health-care-system perspective, health expenditure in the world grew by 36 percent from 2010 to 2017. By contrast, the MENA region grew by approximately 70 percent in the same period. Similarly, from 2010 to 2017, the percentage of out-of-pocket (OOP) expenditure on health-care in the world increased by 36 percent. By contrast, in the MENA region, it increased by 40 percent in the same period.

Therefore, before we delve into the topic of market access, I will give a general overview of the health-care market dynamics that create several challenges but many opportunities as well, from an MA perspective. Although the contents of this book are relevant to all emerging markets, I'll be using the MENA region here as an example of a major emerging market for MNCs in the pharmaceutical industry. These challenges and opportunities call for new approaches and new ways of thinking for MNCs that want to be present in these markets.

From a geographic perspective, I will be referring to WB data in this chapter. The World Bank includes 21 countries in its definition of MENA. However, for the purpose of this book, the focus is on the 17 key markets within the MENA region that share commonalities from a health-system and socio-economic perspective and interconnect in many ways. These 17 countries are Algeria; Bahrain; Egypt; Iraq; Jordan; Kuwait; Lebanon; Libya; Morocco; Oman; Qatar; Saudi Arabia; Syrian Arab Republic; Tunisia; United Arab Emirates (UAE); West Bank and Gaza, Palestine; and Yemen.

The MENA region from a global perspective

According to WB data for 2018, the MENA region makes up 8.8 percent of the size of the world, has 5.9 percent of the world's population, contributes to approximately 4.2 percent of the world's gross domestic product (GDP), has approximately 65 percent of the world's oil reserves, has a significantly higher birth rate compared to the world average, and has a lower crude death rate compared to the world average. **Table 1** shows the numbers for MENA and the world.

Table 1: MENA region key indicators				
Indicator	World	MENA	MENA %	Source
Land (sq. km)	127,343,220	11,232,647	8.8%	WB (2018)
Population (millions)	7,592,886,796	448,912,959	5.9%	WB (2018)
Life expectancy (years)	72.6	74.1	.	WB (2018)
Birth rate (per 1,000)	18.2	22.6	.	WB (2018)
Death rate (crude per 1,000)	7.5	4.9	.	WB (2018)
GDP (current, US $ trillion)	85.9	3.6	4.2%	WB (2018)
Oil Reserve, OPEC (barrels, billion)	79.4%		64.5%	OECD (2018)

If you look at **Table 2** below, which describes key economics and health-care indicators, the population in these 17 countries is approximately 356,786,340 (for the year 2018). The world's population is an estimated 7.6 billion. If you look at GDP per capita, the 17 countries vary significantly with one of the lowest (Yemen) and one of the highest (Qatar) GDPs in the world based on the purchasing power parity (PPP) indicator. If you look at health expenditure per capita, the values also vary significantly from as low as $139 per capita to as high as $3,354 per capita, and everything in between. By comparison, with the world as an indicator, the health expenditure per capita PPP is approximately $1,409. When you look at the OOP expenditure—which is the amount of money that people in countries spend out of their own pockets to buy health-care services—it varies significantly, with some of the markets as low as $106 per capita up to close to $700 per capita.

When you see the total health expenditure in the 17 countries, by simply looking at the total population multiplied by health expenditure per capita, it is equivalent to 111.9 billion US dollars. Out of that, 27.1 billion is spent on pharmaceuticals, which means pharmaceuticals make up about 24 percent of total health expenditure in the region. It's important to note that, according to IQVIA, expenditure on pharmaceuticals in the region has been growing at an estimated 5 to 7 percent compound annual growth rate (CAGR). It's also important to note that the CAGR depends, among other factors, on volatility in oil prices (since most MENA countries are oil-dependent markets) and on currency fluctuation, which is highly relevant to some countries in the region.

To put the health expenditure in the region in perspective, **Figure 1** presents data (based on PPP) that compares MENA to the developed world, including the United States and Europe. Obviously, in the high-income MENA countries (such as Qatar, Kuwait, Saudi Arabia,

Table 2: Economic and health indicators for MENA countries

Country Name	Population 2018	GDP/C, PPP $ 2017	GDP/C, PPP $ 2018	HE/Cap, PPP US$ 2017	HE, OOP, PPP US$ 2017	HE/C Current US$ 2017	LE, total Years 2018	HE, Total Current US$ Tpop*HE/C	Pharm Expend 2017 (US$, Bill)
United Arab Emirates	9,630,959	65,806	67,550	2,469	465.8	1,357	77.8	13,069,379,482	2.7
Bahrain	1,569,439	47,655	47,297	2,265	692.1	1,127	77.2	1,769,050,107	0.4
Algeria	42,228,429	11,551	11,759	975	317.3	258	76.7	10,915,807,908	3.7
Egypt, Arab Rep.	98,423,595	11,014	11,643	614	368.8	106	71.8	10,410,111,628	3.6
Iraq	38,433,600	10,972	10,920	*	*	210	70.5	8,083,112,830	1.8
Jordan	9,956,011	9,841	10,094	757	230.2	341	74.4	3,391,632,670	1.0
Kuwait	4,137,309	50,856	51,708	3,797	479.0	1,529	75.4	6,326,266,668	1.1
Lebanon	6,848,925	16,082	16,417	1,185	393.8	719	78.9	4,927,414,446	1.7
Libya	6,678,567	13,237	14,423	*	*	*	72.7	*	*
Morocco	36,029,138	8,267	8,612	438	236.3	161	76.5	5,801,082,648	1.4
Oman	4,829,483	29,082	29,290	1,591	106.5	588	77.6	2,838,027,822	0.7
West Bank and Gaza	4,569,087	1,599	n/a	*	*	*	73.9	*	*
Qatar	2,781,677	95,058	96,805	3,354	298.6	1,649	80.1	4,587,503,202	0.6
Saudi Arabia	33,699,947	47,309	48,756	2,826	476.5	1,093	75.0	36,847,707,992	7.5
Syrian Arab Republic	16,906,283	*	*	160*	*	*	71.8	*	*
Tunisia	11,565,204	10,608	11,010	863	337.7	251	76.5	2,897,803,251	0.9
Yemen, Rep.	28,498,687	*	*	139*	*	*	66.1	*	*
TOTAL (17 Countries)	356,786,340							111,864,900,653	27.1
World	7,592,886,796	16,176	16,944	1,409	314.8	1,061	72.6	8,056,486,720,353	
Arab World (21 Countries)	419,790,588	14,465	14,887	1,009	329.6	346	71.8	145,159,137,030	

Source: World Bank, IMS, BMI, Market Research (Data accessed June/July 2020)

Figure 1: MENA health expenditures in contrast to other countries

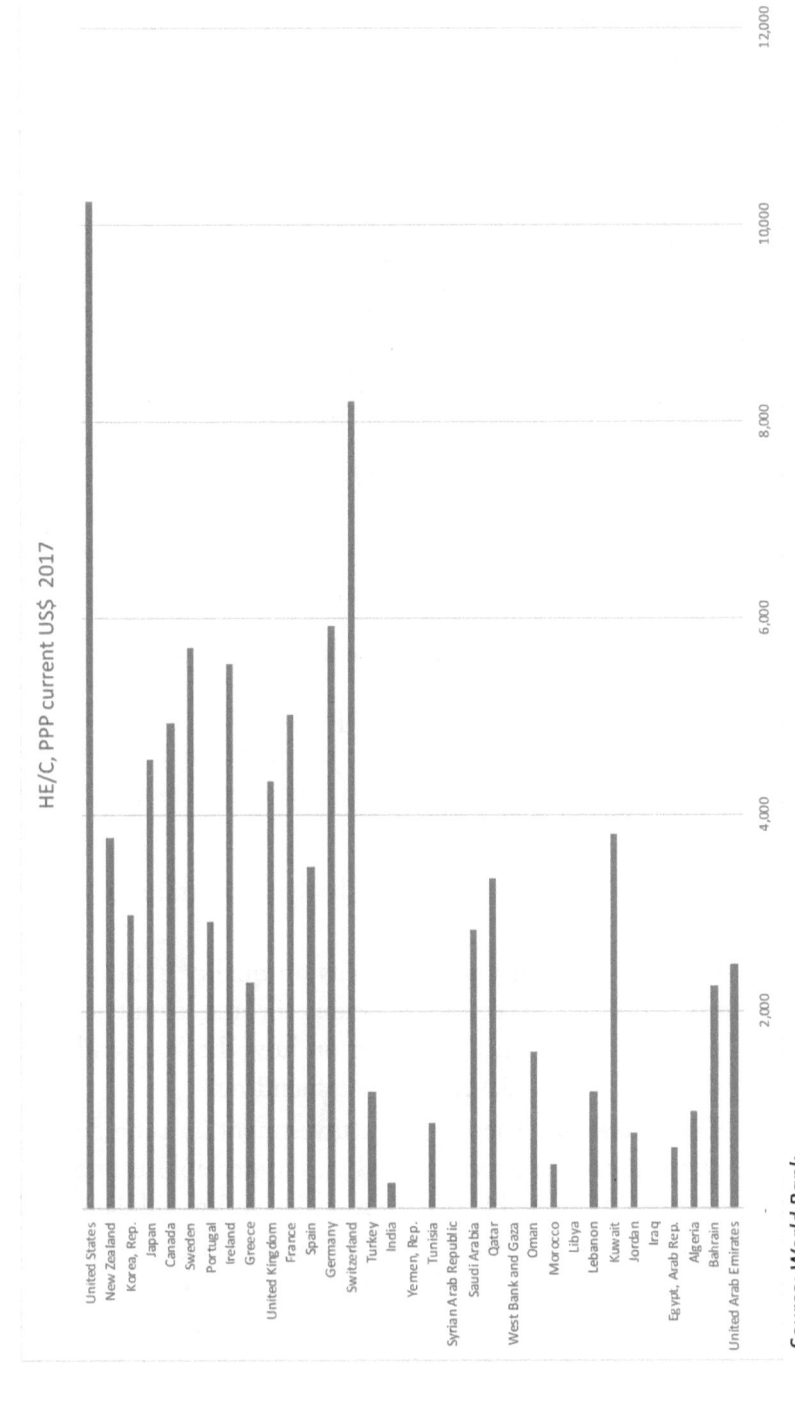

Source: World Bank

and UAE), the health expenditure per capita is approximately that of the Western world. On the other hand, other countries spend far less than their sister countries in the region.

From an overall health-care-system perspective, the MENA markets are highly diverse and so have a diverse system of health-care financing. There are some countries where the government covers public health insurance. There is also a large private health insurance system financed by employers or employer-sponsored plans and, in some markets, a large segment of OOP or self-pay markets. Why does this matter? Because within a country, demographics are changing, and coverage can change from the public sector to private and to OOP, which means patients' level of access to care can vary when they move from one coverage to another. From a pharmaceutical-market perspective, the formulary and the reimbursement will vary significantly between public and private sectors, and obviously for the OOP self-pay market as well. It's also important to keep in mind that these countries interconnect and so reference each other specifically when it comes to pharmaceutical pricing.

Key drivers shaping the future of the health-care system

Several trends are evolving that will shape the future of health-care in the MENA region. These trends will shape the access environment as payers and policy decision-makers use them to control the rising costs of health-care. They include the following:

- **Budget**: There is an increased budget constraint in many countries.
- **Quality**: There is a greater focus on quality indicators and performance measurement as many of the countries introduce pay-for-performance measures on how they're spending and on the outcomes achieved with the spending.
- **Digitalization**: There's greater investment in using digital health, electronic medical records (EMR), and wearable technology, which is contributing to big data or so-called real-world data (RWD).
- **Localization**: There is a greater demand from governments on MNCs for local manufacturing and investment.
- **Speed**: Many countries are requesting faster access to innovations and earlier registration and access to novel therapies.

- **Globalization**: A diffusion of the global trends in health-care is sweeping across the region.
- **Performance**: There is a greater need for showing cost-effectiveness data locally to prove that the innovations brought into the region can deliver on their promises.
- **Transparency**: There are increased calls for legislation around information sharing and increases in inter-country communication between the different health agencies.

From a general pharmaceutical-market perspective, there are several important considerations to highlight:

- For many reasons that are beyond the scope of the current book, MENA is not a research and development-based market. There is very little pharmaceutical R&D in the region.
- Except in some of the large markets, there are no major pharmaceutical manufacturing footprints by MNCs. Many—if not all MNCs—manufacture locally through a contract manufacturing organization or CMO. Of course, there are many local companies (generic producers) that operate in their local markets and some are present regionally.
- From a product-approval perspective, all MENA countries follow what they call "approval by competent health authorities," meaning the products require approval by the United States Food and Drug Administration and/or the European Medicines Agency before it can be registered locally. They will also consider other competent authorities such as the UK National Health System, Health Canada, and/or Swissmedic.
- MENA markets are highly diverse, but because of the culture and the connectedness of the people, many of the economies interconnect and reference each other, especially from a pharmaceutical-pricing perspective.
- In many of the countries, MNCs can only operate through a local distributor and do not have 100 percent ownership of the local enterprise.

Additionally, there are several important challenges in the region, summarized in **Table 3**. These challenges can be grouped into four categories: pricing, innovation, sustainable health-care system, and commercial aspects.

From a **pricing perspective**, international reference pricing (IRP) is one of the main factors contributing to market volatility in the region—which I will explain in Chapter 3—as well as new restrictive procurement practices.

From an **innovation perspective**, intellectual property (IP) and regulatory data protection (RDP) become the key challenges; many of the countries either don't recognize IP rights or, where they recognize them, the enforcement mechanism is not strong. There is also a difficulty when it comes to RDP. Like IP, even where RDP laws exist and are recognized, the enforcement mechanism is weak.

Until recently, long regulatory timelines to drug approval were another problem, but countries have made significant improvements in the last few years and now many have fast-track-approval procedures for innovative breakthrough therapies.

In addition to IP, RDP, and long regulatory timelines, another key challenge from an innovation perspective is the lack of health-care data or the lack of access to the health-care data that countries can use to inform health-care policy. There is a serious lack of disease awareness in many markets and a major lack of epidemiology data on many diseases, especially chronic diseases. There is also a lack of health-care resource-use data, which becomes a big challenge when it comes to conducting health economic evaluations (e.g., cost-effectiveness analyses) to support the value of pharmaceuticals, as I will explain later.

From the perspective of a **sustainable health-care system**, value-based care (VBC) is the main challenge. We will talk more about this in Chapter 4. Suffice to say here, the MENA region is a price-focused market, not a value-based market, despite some recent advancements in some countries in that direction. Also, increased privatization of health-care, cost-shifting toward patients, and increased OOP expenditure have created a real difficulty when it comes to affordability and access to high-value, innovative medicine. The other important challenge from a sustainability standpoint is biosimilars. There is a greater interest in bringing biosimilars to the region; however, there are many countries

The Health-Care and Pharmaceutical Market 29

Table 3: Challenges facing the pharmaceutical industry in the MENA region

Pricing	IRP	References different number of countries with different healthcare systems and values. Major Volatility
	Net price pressure	With budget constraints, there is growing trends toward lower net prices – driven by market competition
	Procurement practices	More stringent procurement measures
Innovation	Regulatory Timelines	Historically, long time for approval (up to 36 months). Recently many countries have Fast Track pathways
	Intellectual Property	This is one of the key challenges in the region; either no IP or no mechanism for IP enforcement is existent.
	Regulatory Data Protection	Similar to IP, this remains a key challenge although some countries are making great strides in this area
	Lack of Health Care Data / Access	This is one of the main challenges. Data is lacking on epidemiology, healthcare resource utilization, etc.
	Disease Awareness	Lack of awareness on many diseases in many areas, especially cancer and chronic diseases
Sustainable Health Care System	Value Based	MENA remains a price-focused market. Although recent initiatives is going in this direction
	Increased Privatization / Cost Shifting	Private sector playing a bigger role. But also greater burden is being put on patients unfortunately as OOP
	Biosimilar Entry	Greater interest on Biosimilar. However, not many guidance on approval yet. But great potential
Commercial Aspects	Parallel Trade	This is one of the main challenges for many markets. Driven by significant price differentials.
	Substandard Generics /Counterfeit	In some markets, this is a key concern, especially sub-standard medicines.
	Local Manufacturing	Some countries require LM for reimbursement.

where the regulatory pathways, or the guidance for introducing biosimilars, are still not there yet. Lastly, MENA is mostly an oil-dependent economy. While this puts many of the countries in the region in the high-income classification, major swings in the price of oil mean significant volatility, which usually increases health expenditure and, ultimately, the expenditure on pharmaceuticals.

From a **commercial perspective**, the key challenges are in three main areas:

1. *Parallel importation (PI)*, driven by large price differences between local and international markets, caused by the pricing regulations in the region (more on this in Chapter 3).
2. *Substandard generics and/or counterfeit.* In some of the markets, substandard generics are a major problem because once a product is introduced to the market, there is no consistent way to test the samples. In some of the markets with political unrest and weak border controls, counterfeit products can easily enter the market along with substandard products.
3. *Local manufacturing (LM) requirements.* Some of the countries mandate local manufacturing as a condition for reimbursement or favor locally manufactured products in public tenders. This becomes a challenge for MNCs for two reasons: first, some of the markets are too small to set up local manufacturing operations; second, considering that most of the pipeline products for MNCs are specialty or biologics, not mass-market products, there is a tendency now to combine operations, not expand them, to ensure efficiency and reduce manufacturing costs.

Despite these challenges and market volatility, the MENA region is still a growth market because of these unique opportunities:

1. *Population growth.* MENA has one of the fastest-growing populations worldwide and the percentage of the population under the age of 25 is the highest in the world—although the segment of the population that is 60 years and above is growing rapidly, which has significant implications on future demand for chronic medicine.

2. *A brand-loyal market.* Most countries import branded pharmaceutical products because more patients trust them. In fact, in many of the markets, imported products make up 80 percent of the pharmaceutical market by value.
3. *An attractive market for MNCs.* From an overall economic, consumer, and patient-sentiment perspective, there is a high demand for new technologies, products, and services, and consumers have a high expectation that they will receive prompt access to such innovation.

Impact on market access

What is the relevance of the above background from a pharmaceutical MA standpoint? There are several important considerations:

1. The overall political, socio-economic, and health-care systems of a country play a major role in attracting MNCs to the region.
2. Senior management's understanding of the region will help them deal with the volatility and take a long-term view of the market rather than deal with its short-term volatility.
3. MA, strategic planning, and execution are now the most critical factors in the commercial success of innovative therapies coming to markets. The complexity of the markets, connectivity, and cross-country influence collectively mean that anything short of excellence in the MA approach will not only lead to suboptimal performance and failure but also cause further market volatility.
4. With most development pipelines in the industry in specialty pharmaceuticals, biologics, and assets targeting rare diseases, affordability and budget impact will be a challenge, especially in OOP markets. MNCs need to be prepared in terms of the target markets they operate in to develop the right MA approach to each market.
5. There is a shift from public to private insurance and increased patient costs as OOP co-payments. There is also a growing interest in achieving universal health insurance. The hope is that the direct OOP payment spent now will contribute to insur-

ance premiums, so as not to further increase the cost burden on patients.

6. From a financial perspective, players in the region are getting interested in pay for performance (P4P) measures and outcomes-based agreements (OBAs) as a way of driving greater attention toward patient outcomes, as well as functioning as a cost-containment measure to drive efficiency in the health-care system.

These considerations for MNCs imply that pharmaceutical companies need to take a new approach to collaboration with stakeholders in the health-care ecosystem (the 4 Ps: policymakers, payers, providers, and patients or patient advocacy groups). Key aspects to collaborate on are policies to ensure that the rules and regulations of the health-care system are progressive enough for easy access to care, to streamline operations in the market to drive efficiency, and to drive greater private-public partnerships. The goal is a sustainable health-care system.

Summary

The MENA health-care system is diverse. Several factors contribute to the huge demand for health-care, a demand that is putting pressure on the health-care system. While there are many serious challenges in the MENA region, there are many great opportunities as well. In the upcoming chapters, I will focus on the critical elements needed to develop the right MA strategy and the key skill sets that MA professionals should master to become successful in their role.

Lastly, and more importantly, this is not all about the commercial opportunity for MNCs that operate in the region. **Failure to develop successful MA strategies means that patients in emerging markets in general and the MENA region, in particular, will suffer because of delayed launch (or no launch) of innovative life-saving therapies.** Partial access to therapies by only those patients who can afford them can create an imbalance in socio-economic status, leading to social instability and unsustainability in the health-care system. The results will be worse social, economic, and health indicators (the health indicators are reduced mortality rate, improved life expectancy, reduced comorbidities), and overall reduced productivity.

2

THE WINNING MARKET ACCESS MINDSET

What is market access?

According to the World Trade Organization (WTO), "Market access for goods means the conditions, tariffs and non-tariff measures, agreed by members for the entry of specific goods into their markets."

As per the World Health Organization (WHO) framework for health-care systems, "A well-functioning health system ensures equitable access to essential medical products, vaccines, and technologies of assured quality, safety, efficacy, and cost-effectiveness, and their scientifically sound and cost-effective use."

From a pharmaceutical perspective, we can define market access as the availability of medicines to the right patient population, to as many patients as possible, in as many countries as possible, and in a sustainable way. Given that the pharmaceutical industry is heavily regulated, this definition applies to the locally approved indications of the product.

A strategic approach to market access

As illustrated in **Figure 2**, there are five steps to the strategic approach to market access:

Figure 2: Strategic approach to market access throughout product life cycle

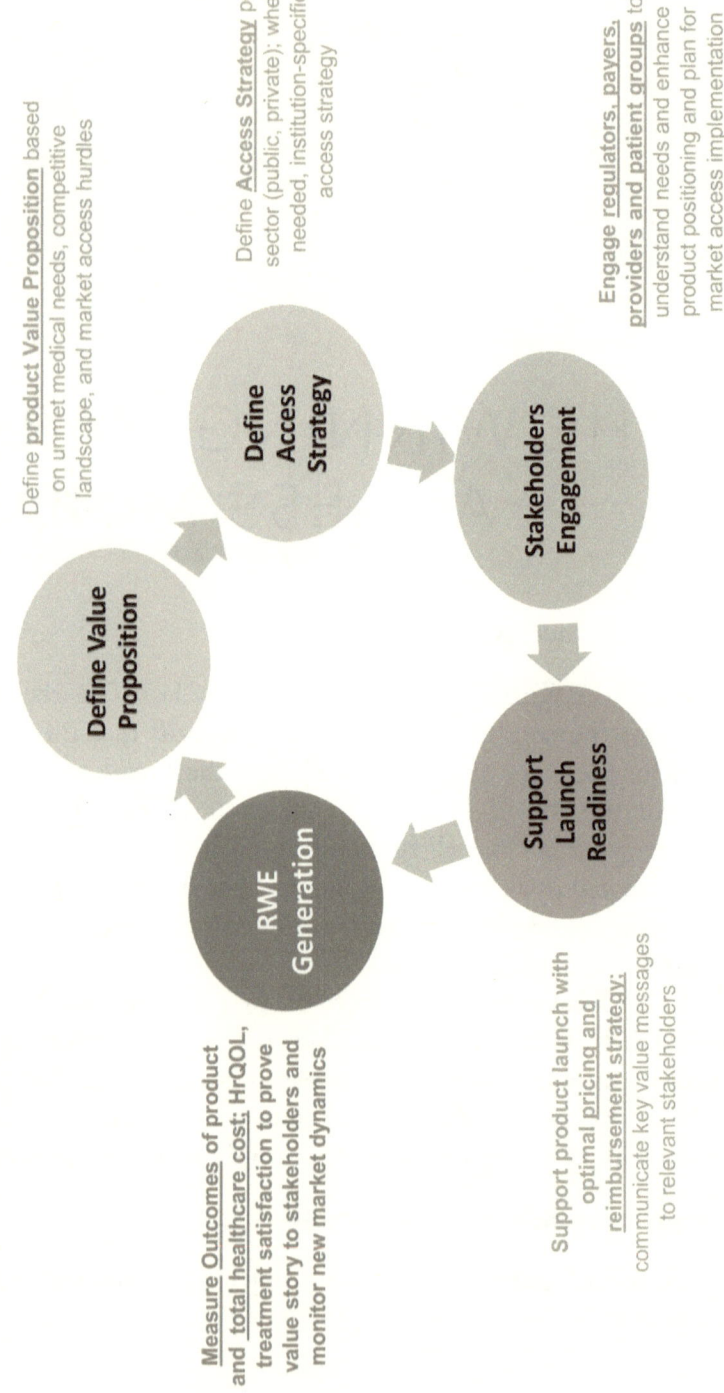

1. **Define the value proposition**: This step includes defining the product value proposition based on its pharmacology, currently available therapies, disease priority, and the unmet medical needs of the market.
2. **Define the access strategy**: Here, the type of access strategy for the different sectors of the market (e.g., private, public, institution-specific) depends on where there is potential for the product.
3. **Engage stakeholders**: In this step, what is needed is an early engagement of the regulators, payers, providers, and patient groups, to understand their needs, enhance product positioning, and plan for MA implementation.
4. **Support the product launch:** Here, what is needed is to support the product launch with the optimal pricing and reimbursement strategy early on, and to communicate the key value messages (KVM) to all stakeholders.
5. **Generate RWD and real-world evidence (RWE)**: This is to document the outcomes associated with the product and its impact on the total health-care cost, its potential impact on patients' health-related quality of life (HrQOL), and treatment satisfaction.

What does a market access mindset in an organization entail?

The MA mindset entails a coordinated approach across those functions in the organization responsible for the development and commercialization of the product. Market access is at the center of the cross-functional teams and leads the access-related activities of the medical affairs, regulatory affairs, government affairs and policy, and commercial teams (including business unit, key account management, and finance). This coordinated approach must continue throughout the product life cycle (which I will further explain in Chapter 5), but it is especially important at the pre-launch phase of new products. **Figure 3** illustrates the coordinated approach to market access.

When you look at the four key functions, starting with medical affairs, the MA function needs to work with medical affairs on evidence generation and value communication. The medical affairs function needs

Figure 3: Coordinated approach to market access

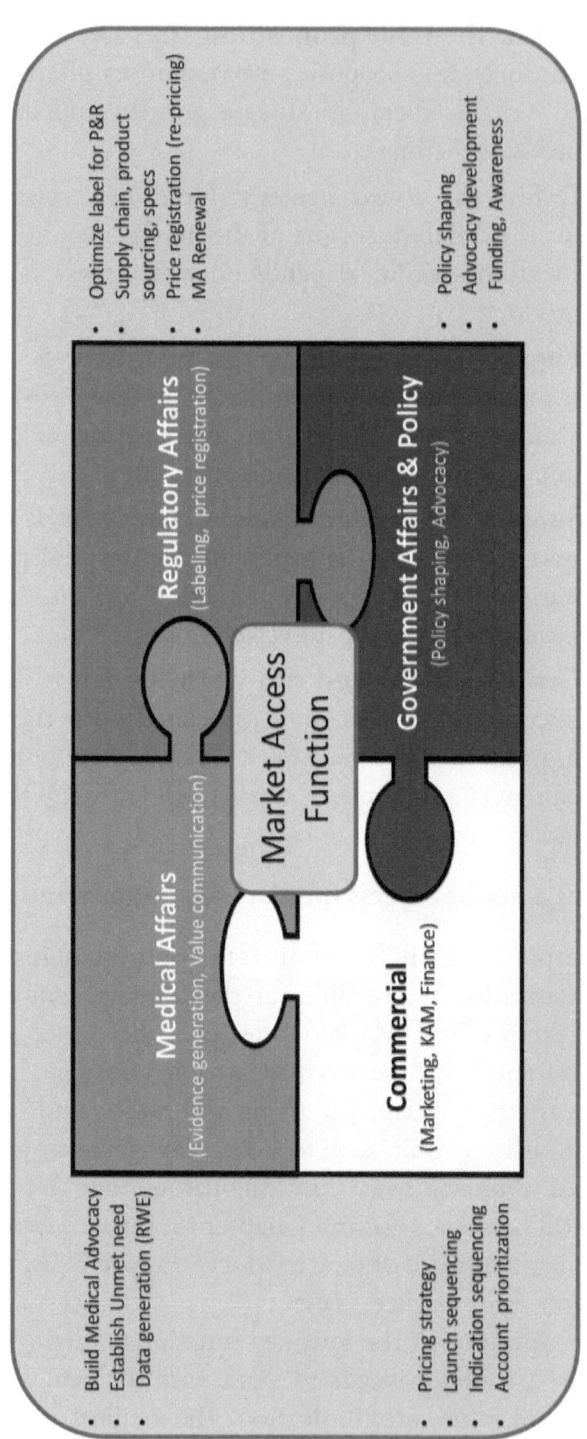

to ensure that the right medical advocacy is strong. There must be leading clinicians, key opinion leaders, and key medical decision-makers within the prominent institutions where the product will go for a formulary listing to prove the high unmet medical need of the product. The medical affairs function needs to generate the data from clinical trials, or plan prospective data collection, to substantiate the value the product brings to the market. The MA function needs to work closely with regulatory affairs to ensure the best labeling of the product, and closely coordinate with them when it comes to price registration and preparation of the price certificate, which is part of the regulatory file. Specifically, the goal should be to optimize the label from a pricing and reimbursement perspective, which also includes close coordination with the supply chain on product sourcing. Working with regulatory affairs to ensure price registration is seamless is important at the product's first launch, but even more important when repricing products upon market authorization renewal (MAR) to mitigate, as much as possible, the impact of IRP on the future price of the product.

The MA function also needs to work closely with government affairs and policy on policy shaping and advocacy development, specifically around the rules and regulations governing key aspects of the pharmaceutical market, including IP, RDP, pricing, reimbursement, health-care financing, and disease awareness. It needs to build advocacy, especially in therapeutic areas where the product soon to be launched has not been well established, or where significant access hurdles exist that could lead to delayed or restricted reimbursement. It also needs to cooperate closely to ensure that the right funding mechanism for a new therapy is available.

When it comes to commercial functions, the MA function needs to work collaboratively with all aspects of the commercial organization—most importantly, the marketing team, the KAM team, and the finance team. Early alignment between the market access, commercial, and global teams on launch sequencing is critically important to managing the following vital aspects:

- The perceived value of the product by payers, based on the availability of data at launch.
- Optimization of pricing strategy, especially given the complex

IRP system that MENA countries use.
- Indication sequencing for products with multiple indications, which also has a direct impact on pricing strategy, but more importantly from a payer budget-impact perspective.

When the right MA mindset is embedded in the organization, the result is the successful launch and uptake of the product. **Figure 4** illustrates the importance of having the right MA mindset at product launch. The graph depicts the launch of three different products:

1. **Product A (solid line)**: Here, the company does not have the right MA strategy, or it had the right MA strategy but did not execute it well. It is well accepted that both formulary access and reimbursement during the first eight quarters after launch are critical because they will define the future success of the product. You can see on the graph where this product only achieved 40 percent of its target reimbursement potential. After that, the product only reached 50 percent of its potential by its fourth year on the market.
2. **Product B (dotted line):** Here, the company did a better job in planning or executing its MA strategy but was able to achieve only 20 percent of its formulary access potential by the fourth quarter after launch, and the product achieved only 50 percent of its potential by the eighth quarter after launch. Subsequently, the product achieved only 75 percent of its potential by its fourth year on the market.
3. **Product C (dashed line).** This is the optimal case of MA where both the planning and execution of the company paid off. The product achieved 20 percent of its target formulary listing by the second quarter and achieved 50 percent by the fifth quarter post-launch, and by the eighth quarter after launch, the product was formulary listed in more than 80 percent of the target accounts.

Therefore, it is critical to embed the right MA mindset in the organization. This will ensure that the execution of the strategies will lead to the best uptake and the right product trajectory in terms of future market growth.

Figure 4: Impact of market access planning and execution on product launch

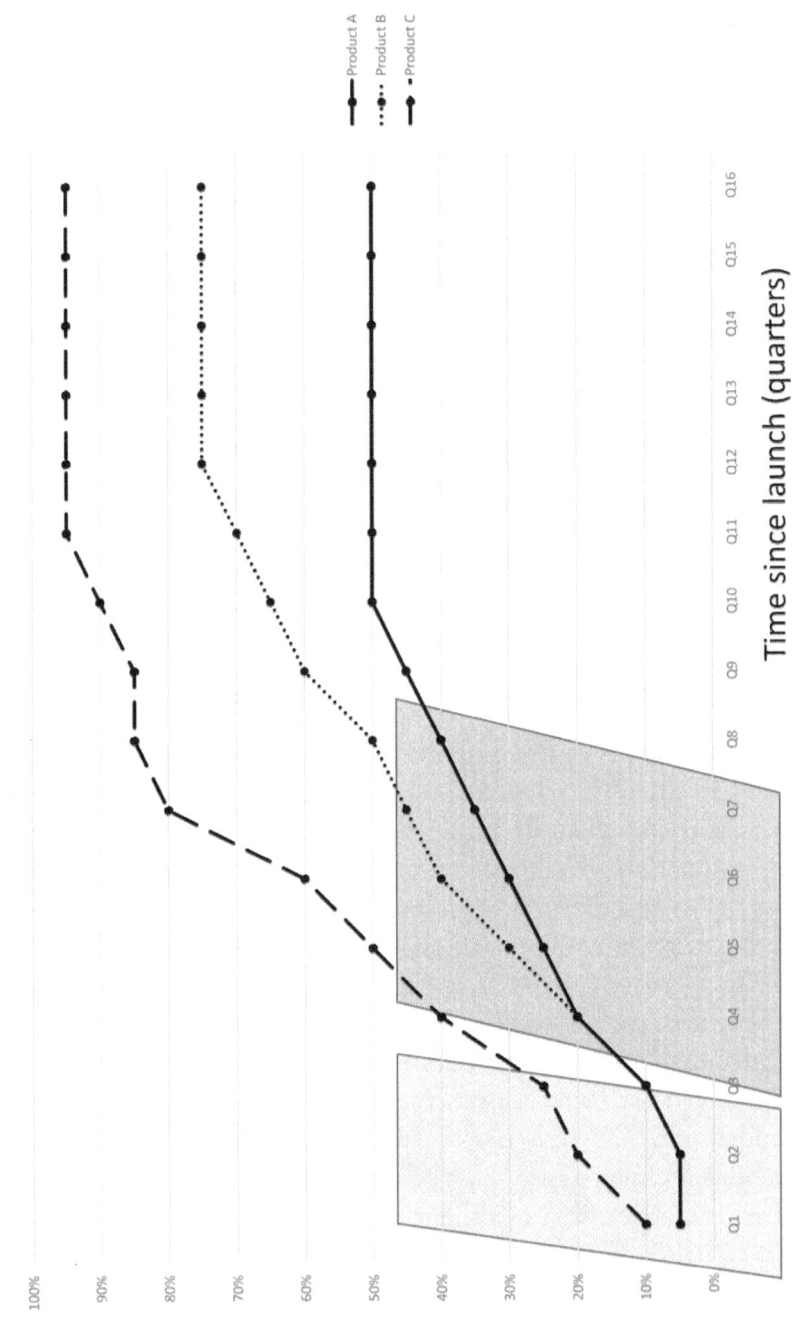

The strategic approach to market access

For a company with the right MA mindset to be successful, it also needs to focus on two key strategies. The first is to ensure that all activities focus on the five key pillars of market access (see **Figure 5**); the second is to have the right stakeholder engagement, which focuses on value creation with payers in the health-care system.

As illustrated in **Figure 5**, the first major activity that the company should focus on, from an MA perspective, is setting the best pricing strategy throughout the product life cycle. This is one of the most critical steps that the MA function, as a lead for the organization, must take to be successful.

The second major activity is to secure reimbursement and formulary listing of the product in the key sectors (private, public) and/or key institutional accounts.

The third is to optimize access and remove restrictions where the product is already reimbursed or on the formulary, but with restrictions. The focus here should be on how to remove restrictions to allow the maximum number of eligible patients for the approved indication to have access to the product.

The fourth is to drive uptake (also known as the adoption of innovation) in the target patient population as per labeled indication. This situation arises when the product is sub-optimally used in the right patient population for different reasons. In that case, key activities should focus on how to drive the uptake to ensure that the product delivers on its promise and its value to the health-care system.

The final step relates to the days of therapy that patients are taking the product. In this case, the product is optimally reimbursed in that patient population and prescribing the product to the right patient population—yet for some reason, the duration of therapy is not as per the intended use. The activities should focus on generating data that convince stakeholders of the value of staying on therapy for longer as per the labeled indication and treatment duration. The activities should also focus on interventions that enhance long-term adherence and compliance to the product.

From an organizational perspective, depending on whether the company has separate MA and HEOR functions, the HEOR function

Figure 5: The five key pillars of successful market access strategy
All MA activities should fall into one of these FIVE categories

can focus on generating evidence to support the value dossier while the MA function can focus on pre-launch and post-launch activities, working closely with the commercial organization. Obviously, where the MA and the HEOR departments are the same, then the same group will do these activities. Either way, success depends on close cooperation and coordination.

From a stakeholder-management perspective, as illustrated in **Figure 6**, there are four key steps to payer engagement. These steps focus on value creation from a customer or payer-engagement perspective.

The first step is to listen and understand the needs and the concerns of the payers as a key stakeholder, including identifying the key challenges, concerns, and what the payer objectives are—because it's vital to align payer needs with the objectives of the company. I will explain this further in Chapter 8 when we discuss negotiations.

The second step is to confirm and prioritize the needs. Here, the goal is to align the payer needs with the company objectives and product value strategy and what it brings to the health-care system.

The third is to design the right value solution—to develop an integrated value solution based on the priorities identified and the promise of the product value proposition that will materialize to the payers and patients.

The fourth is to develop performance measures. Many of the payers have key performance indicators (KPIs) they want to achieve. So, it's very important to develop and implement the right KPIs that can support payer performance.

Summary

A winning MA mindset means that the MA team is customer-oriented. Its knowledge of the business model of its customers ensures it can deliver customer-specific win-win solutions that solve unique settings or problems and deliver excellence in the execution of MA plans. It is also where all the cross-functional teams in the company align with the critical success factors and key activities to achieve the defined MA strategy.

Now that I have explained the importance of having a winning MA mindset, the next chapter will focus on the importance of not only understanding pricing but, more importantly, how to manage pricing as a key strategy to maximize access and drive the growth of the company.

Figure 6: Approach to stakeholders engagement on value creation

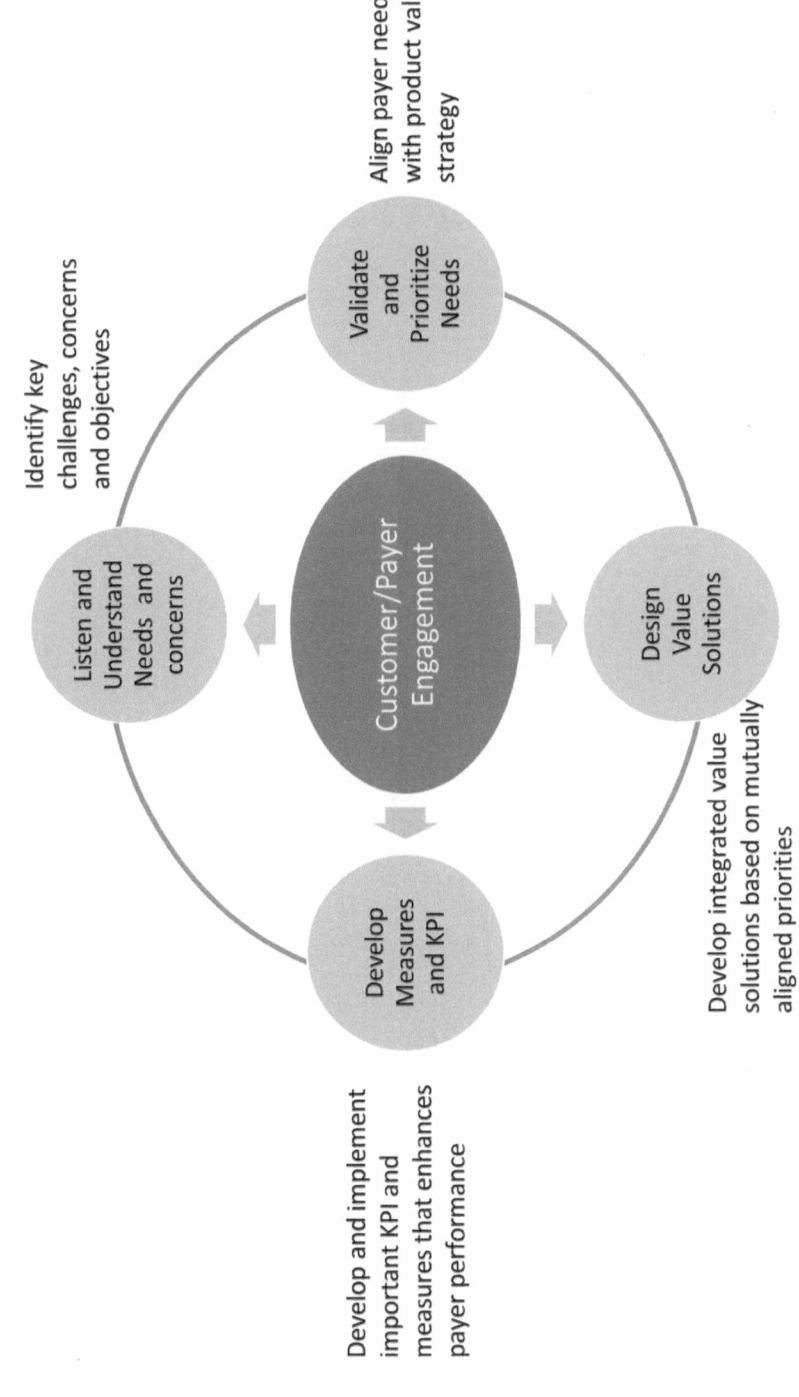

3

PRICING AND MARKET ACCESS

In this chapter, I will cover pricing, one of the most critical aspects of market access. I will be focusing on:

- definitions and key terms
- mechanisms used in setting the prices of pharmaceuticals
- determinants and considerations used in pricing and reimbursement
- impact of launch sequencing on pricing
- critical success factors in managing pricing volatility.

Definitions and key terms

Ex-factory price: Defined as the price set by the manufacturer as the product exits the factory. Usually, it excludes taxes.

CIF price: Standing for cost, insurance, and freight, it is the price at the point of entry to the receiving country, also referred to as the product's list price registered at the Ministry of Health (MOH).

FOB price: Standing for freight on board, it refers to the price that the company sells the product for to a third-party licensed purchaser. It means the purchaser will pay for the shipping and customs clearance of the goods.

Net price: Defined as the price after any discount, free-of-charge (FOC) goods, distributor commission, and taxes paid. It's the price that the company uses in its profit and loss (P&L) statement.

Wholesale price: Defined as the price that the licensed distributor or importer sells to retailers, institutions, and/or governments. It usually includes distributor commission and/or other applicable charges. It is usually the price used or reported regularly in the inflation index.

Public selling price: This is the price paid by the end-user—the consumer/the patient (i.e., the price at the pharmacy)—usually inclusive of all taxes, if applicable, distributor commission, and pharmacy margins.

It is important to understand the difference between the definitions because of the direct impact on the P&L statement and, more importantly, for price-setting at the time of product registration, as some countries register with CIF price while others register with FOB. Also, some countries have specific rules on which price to quote when quoting prices for the tender.

In addition to the key definitions, there are some important pricing processes to understand:

Price vetting: This is the pricing research done to decide the best price for a product. The company usually does this when it is about to launch a product, and they do it with different stakeholders—with the prospective payers or payer advisors and with potential prescribers to understand their feelings about the price, compared to the perceived value of the product. In formal or advanced pricing research, this generally involves price elasticity studies to assess the willingness to pay (WTP) of the public and private sector (and potentially, patients in OOP markets) to figure out the price that would maximize the commercial opportunity.

Price-setting: This is the process used to decide the pricing strategy internally, within the company, to set the ex-factory price of the product in different regions using the so-called price band or price corridor in different countries. It usually takes into consideration the reference prices used by different countries, which I will explain in the next section, the socio-economic status of different countries, the types of health-care systems, and the WTP of the different payers.

Price netting: This is the process of setting net prices (also known as floor price) in different countries or different accounts or channels within the country to enhance the product's commercial opportunity.

Price netting is used in tender management, in establishing confidential net prices in different accounts or key institutions, and/or in addressing affordability programs, which I will explain in Chapter 6.

Mechanisms used in setting the prices of pharmaceuticals

There are several pharmaceutical-pricing mechanisms used globally to set ex-manufacturer prices. These include the following:

Free pricing: The company decides where to set the ex-factory price of the product. The United States is the most widely used example of a country that uses this pricing mechanism.

International reference pricing (IRP): Sometimes also referred to as external reference pricing (ERP), it is the most widely used mechanism by countries to set the ex-factory prices of pharmaceutical products. It considers the prices of the same product in the reference countries. This is the mechanism used in all MENA countries to set the price of pharmaceuticals, as I will explain later in this chapter.

Value-based pricing (VBP): This is the pricing mechanism used to set the prices based on the value of the product to the payer or to the health-care system. It is a relatively new mechanism of price-setting, used mostly in countries that use formal health technology assessment (HTA) to set their prices and in countries with single-payer systems with national reimbursement. However, more recently, some institutions or channels in MENA have started using VBP in their reimbursement decisions.

Indication-based pricing: This is the mechanism whereby the same product receives different prices for different indications, usually during reimbursement negotiations between the company and different payers. It's important to note that all countries in the MENA region follow IRP to set the prices of their pharmaceuticals and no country in the region currently uses indication-based pricing.

From a MENA perspective, **Figure 7** illustrates the reference countries used for price-setting in the different countries. As illustrated, MENA countries reference anywhere from 5 to 36 countries when it comes to price-setting. It's important to note that these reference countries used by MENA are very different. They have different health-care-system values, socio-economic statuses, and health-care capabilities. As a rule, most MENA countries take the lowest price in the reference countries when setting their ex-factory price locally. Only Jordan and the

48 Frontiers in Market Access

Figure 7: Reference countries used in IRP in MENA countries

Saudi Arabia 30 Lowest	Egypt 36 Lowest	Syria	Oman 30 Lowest	Bahrain 30 Lowest	Lebanon 14 Lowest	Jordan 20 Median	Iraq	Kuwait 30 Lowest	Qatar 5 Lowest	Yemen	UAE 18 Median	Algeria 9 Lowest -10%	Morocco 7 Lowest	Tunisia Lowest	Libya
Algeria	Algeria		Algeria	Algeria				Algeria						Algeria	
Australia	Austria		Australia	Australia		Austria		Australia			Austria				
Argentina	Argentina		Argentina	Argentina		Azerbaijan		Argentina							
Bahrain	Bahrain		Bahrain	Bahrain	Bahrain			Bahrain		Bahrain	Bahrain				
Belgium	Belgium		Belgium	Belgium	Belgium	Belgium	Belgium	Belgium		Belgium	Belgium	Belgium	Belgium		
Canada	Canada		Canada	Canada		Bulgaria		Canada			Canada				
Cyprus	Cyprus		Cyprus	Cyprus		Croatia		Cyprus							
						Cyprus									
Denmark	Denmark		Denmark	Denmark		Czech Rep		Denmark			Denmark				
Egypt	Egypt		Egypt	Egypt				Egypt							
	Finland										Finland				
France	France		France	France	France	France	France	France			France	France	France	France	
Germany	Germany		Germany	Germany		Georgia		Germany			Germany			Germany	
Greece	Greece		Greece	Greece		Greece	Greece	Greece				Greece			
Hungary	Hungary		Hungary	Hungary		Hungary		Hungary							
Ireland	Ireland		Ireland	Ireland		Ireland		Ireland			Ireland				
	India														
	Iran														
Italy	Italy		Italy	Italy	Italy	Italy	Italy	Italy			Italy			Italy	
Japan	Japan		Japan	Japan				Japan							
Jordan	Jordan		Jordan	Jordan	Jordan		Jordan	Jordan							
Kuwait	Kuwait		Kuwait	Kuwait	Kuwait		Kuwait		Kuwait		Kuwait				
Lebanon	Lebanon	Lebanon	Lebanon	Lebanon		Lebanon		Lebanon							
	Morocco											Morocco		Morocco	
New Zealand	New Zealand		New Zealand	New Zealand		New Zealand		New Zealand			Netherland				
Netherland	Netherland		Netherland	Netherland			Netherland	Netherland			Norway				
	Norway														
Oman	Oman			Oman	Oman			Oman	Oman						
	Philippine														
	Poland														
Portugal	Portugal		Portugal	Portugal	Portugal	Portugal		Portugal				Portugal	Portugal		
					Qatar			Qatar	Qatar						
						Romania									
						Slovenia									
Spain	Spain		Spain	Spain	Spain	Spain	Spain	Spain			Spain	Spain	Spain	Spain	
Saudi Arabia	Saudi Arabia		Saudi Arabia	Saudi Arabia	Saudi Arabia	Saudi Arabia*	Saudi Arabia	Saudi Arabia	Saudi Arabia		Saudi Arabia		Saudi Arabia		
	Sudan														
South Korea			South Korea	South Korea				South Korea							
Sweden	Sweden		Sweden	Sweden				Sweden			Sweden				
Switzerland	Switzerland		Switzerland	Switzerland	Switzerland		Switzerland	Switzerland			Switzerland				
Turkey	Turkey		Turkey	Turkey				Turkey				Turkey	Turkey		
						Tunisia						Tunisia			Tunisia
UAE	UAE		UAE	UAE	UAE			UAE	UAE						
UK	UK		UK	UK	UK		UK	UK			UK				

UAE take the median price of the reference countries. Once the price is set (by the MOH in most countries), the price is fixed for five years, which is essentially the market authorization period of the product. The only exception to that is Jordan, where, in the first registration of a new product, the price is fixed for two years, and then it goes through re-pricing to allow for lower prices as more reference countries launch the product; then the price is fixed for five years.

More recently, the UAE also introduced a similar mechanism where the price of the product for the first registration is fixed for 18 months, then repriced and fixed for five years.

With the growing interest in cost-effectiveness analysis, some countries in the region have started using it in price-setting. Currently, only Saudi Arabia, Jordan, and Egypt have formal references in their pricing rules on how companies can use cost-effectiveness analysis to support their price request. However, it is not used widely in the region and even in these three countries, where the rule formally references cost-effectiveness, it's not mandatory to use it in price-setting—although it is useful to have.

Determinants and considerations used in pricing and reimbursement

Now that we have covered the key pricing definitions and mechanisms, let's discuss the key considerations used in setting the price of innovative pharmaceutical products. As you can see in **Figure 8**, there are seven factors used when setting the price of an innovative pharmaceutical product. Of these seven factors, six are directly related to the health-care system, and only one is related to the overall socio-economic system of the country.

As illustrated in this figure, the starting point is the value proposition of the new product—that is, the product's value proposition based on its pharmacologic property, target product profile, and the unmet medical needs in the specific disease state where the product will be used (and other indications in case multiple indications are targeted).

The next consideration is the value of the product, given the competitors in the marketplace that are available and the incremental value the product brings above and beyond what is currently available in the market.

After that, comes WTP, where the incremental value that the payer

50 Frontiers in Market Access

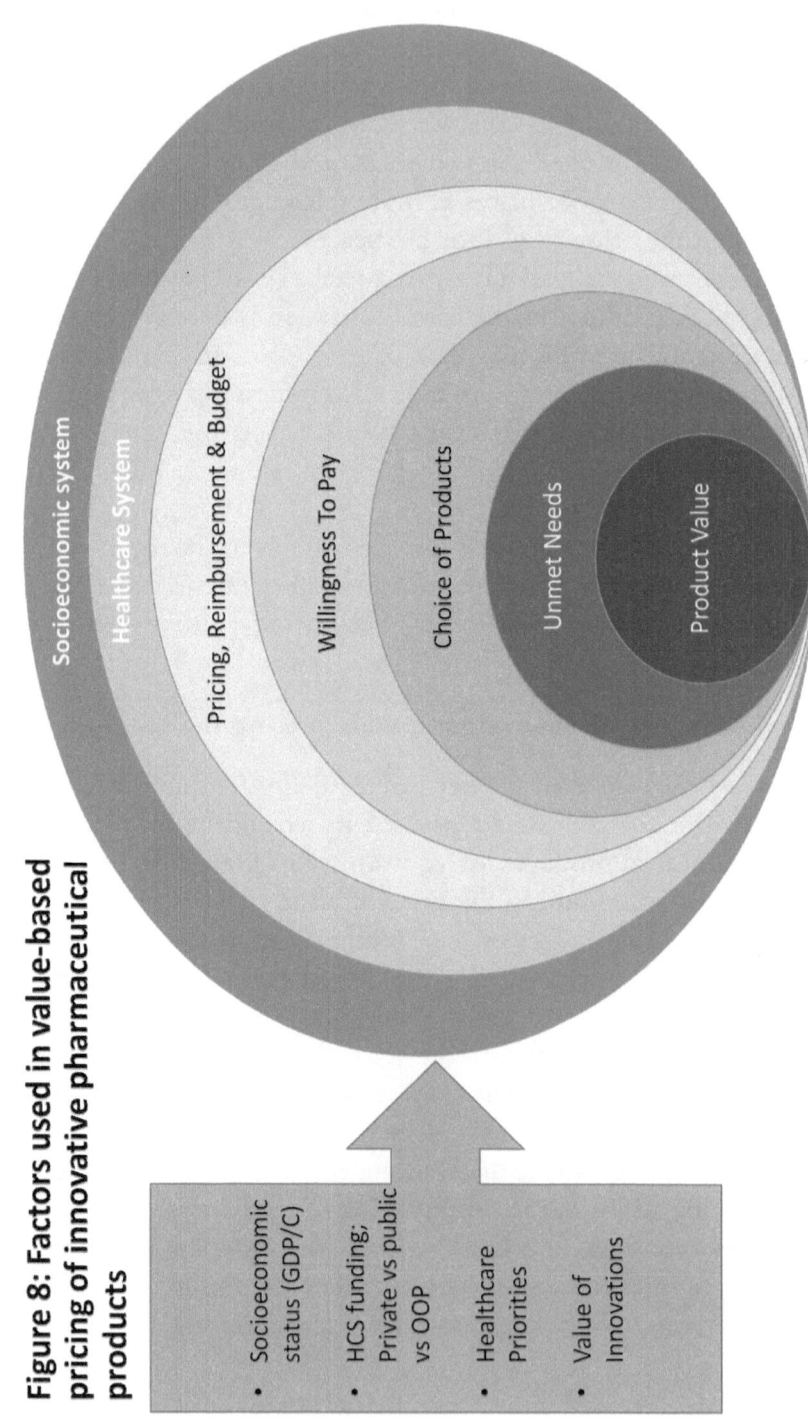

Figure 8: Factors used in value-based pricing of innovative pharmaceutical products

is willing to pay for the added benefit is taken into consideration based on the incremental expected value of the product above and beyond what is currently available, given the unmet medical need.

The next considerations are pricing, reimbursement, and budget impact. What is the impact on the total pharmaceutical budget, given the current market dynamics and expected usage pattern?

The last consideration from a direct health-care-system perspective is the overall impact on the socio-economic system of the country, where total health expenditure is considered, given the value of the product to the overall health-care system. This is especially important in countries with a single-payer social system.

In this context, a country usually conducts a formal value assessment of the product, performing cost-effectiveness analyses to prove the clinical and economic value of the product. Usually, cost-effectiveness is from a payer perspective. The direct medical-care costs are taken into consideration, and then the indirect medical costs are presented in sensitivity analyses to figure out the value of the product from a societal perspective.

It is important to point out that cost-effectiveness analysis is only one consideration in the decision-making process of the value of the product and should not be the only consideration. Other considerations include socio-economic parameters of the different countries, in terms of GDP per capita, the type of health-care system and the funding mechanism, the health-care priorities in the countries, and how the innovative product fits into the health-care priorities of the policymakers in the countries, and how different countries value innovations.

The price and the value

What is the relationship between price and value? There are three important aspects to this question:

1. Price reflects value—price is what the patient (or payer) pays, and value is what they get for the price they pay.
2. Value means different things to different stakeholders (to the payer, provider or prescriber, and to patients).
3. Different stakeholders perceive the value of a product differently.

These are important considerations in the context of pricing, reimbursement, and access.

Figure 9 illustrates the triangle of the key factors that affect the value perception:

1. *The value dossier:* The value dossier conveys the clinical, economic, and humanistic value of the product based on the approved label. It is supposed to articulate, concisely and effectively, to formulary decision-makers and reimbursement authorities the value that the product brings to their institution (or to the government).
2. *The regulations landscape:* This involves knowing and understanding the reimbursement environment—that is, the guidelines (e.g., pharmacoeconomics), rules and regulations commonly used in the institutions (or governments), the requirements for submissions, and the available data for constructing the value proposition.
3. *Stakeholder engagement:* The ongoing relationship with policy-makers, payers, professional societies, and patient groups, and whether the company has strong advocacy and support for their position and the value of the product.

These factors have the following important strategic and operational considerations, which the company needs to manage:

- a well-thought-out pricing strategy to cover ex-factory price, net price, and tender strategy
- careful launch sequencing—this is important to minimize the potential negative exposure of IRP
- a comprehensive MA strategy by the different market archetypes, as I will explain in detail in Chapter 5
- availability of affordability programs to address OOP and self-pay markets
- strategy for RWE generation to show the value of the product after its introduction to the market.

Figure 9: Factors that impact the value perception of products

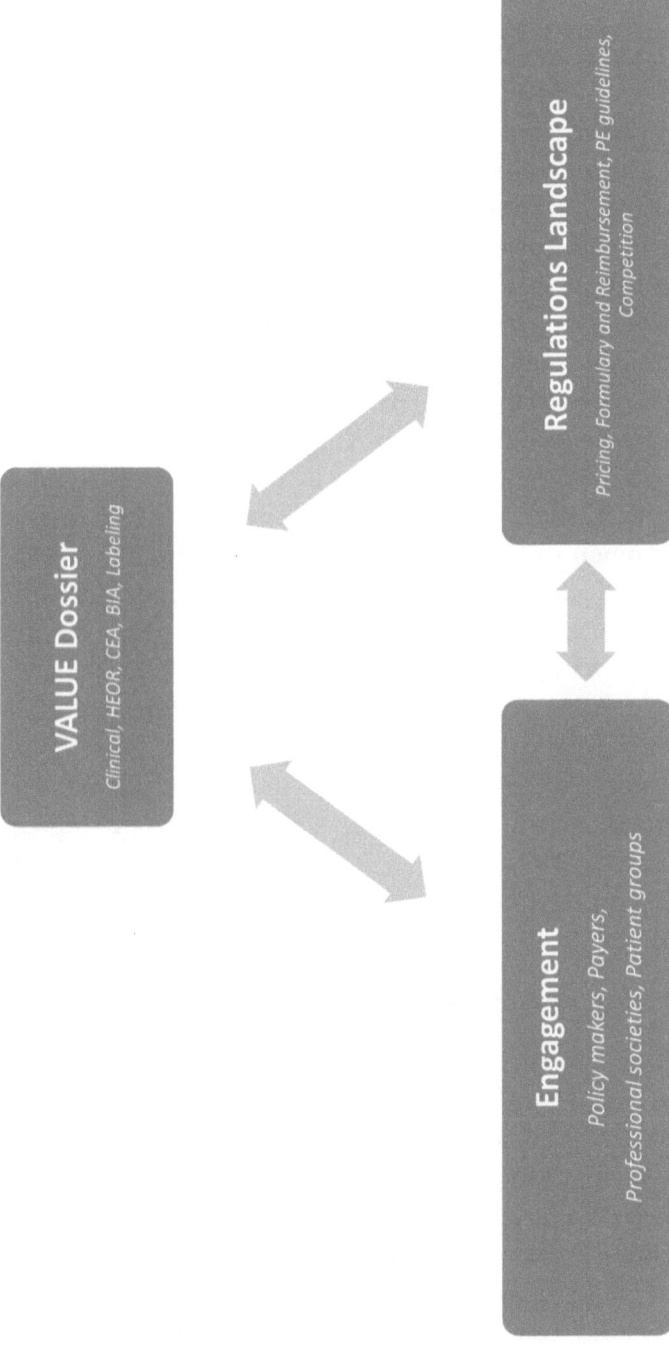

Impact of launch sequencing on pricing

Given that the MENA countries use the IRP mechanism for price-setting, carefully managing launch sequencing becomes a critical success factor to optimize the ex-factory prices in the different countries. I can best illustrate this point by using **Figure 10**, which is a hypothetical example of how to set the ex-factory price of a product in Jordan, where the IRP system is used. As a reminder, Jordan uses the lowest price of either the price in Saudi Arabia or the median of the reference countries (and reprices the product after two years from initial approval).

As illustrated in the figure, in this hypothetical example, the product is launched in France, Germany, Greece, Hungary, Italy, Portugal, Slovenia, Spain, and the United Kingdom (which are the countries formally included in the list of reference countries for Jordan) at the indicated timelines and respective prices. What's important to note is that Jordan will launch the new product in the third quarter of 2022. Since Jordan takes the price as the median of the reference price countries, the expected ex-factory price based on the IRP rule, given the different prices in reference countries, is $1,500. Knowing that Jordan will have to reprice the product in the first two years after launch, and since there is a new country that's coming in with a lower price, then the expected price at the time of renewal in the third quarter of 2024 (two years after first approval) will be $1,450. This is important for two practical reasons: 1) to include in the long-range planning that companies use in their budgeting process; 2) to plan for IRP where Jordan is a reference country to minimize price volatility.

How do we ensure optimal launch sequencing?

First and foremost, from a commercial perspective, the global project team (GPT)—working very closely with the regional and/or country commercial team and the business unit head (BUH) in the region—should align the countries in the different waves of the launch (Wave 1, Wave 2, Wave 3, etc.), based on several factors, one of which is the optimization of the pricing strategy. Once the GPT makes the strategic decision on the launch waves, the commercial team should move into the execution phase and launch readiness. This includes working with the regulatory affairs team to prepare the dossier as well as collaborating with

Figure 10: Impact of launch sequence on price setting – example

Example: Launch sequence for a new product launch in Jordan

		1Q2021	2Q2021	3Q2021	4Q2021	1Q2022	2Q2022	3Q2022	4Q2022	1Q2023	2Q2023	3Q2023	4Q2023	1Q2024	2Q2024	3Q2024	4Q2024
IRP Countries	France	1800															
	Greece				1400												
	Hungary								1100								
	Italy			1500													
	Portugal				1400												
	Slovenia						1300										
	Spain			1600													
	UK		1600														
New Launch	Jordan							1500								1450	

Key Considerations
- Carefully plan launch sequence to minimize re-pricing and mitigate impact on the P&L.
- Manage IRP carefully to avoid delay in launching products in low-price markets.

the MA and pricing teams to prepare the price certificate, which is part of the dossier submitted to the pricing department within the MOH. Lastly, from a supply-chain perspective, the teams must work closely to align product sourcing and availability at the time of launch. This is important because the country of origin (COO) is critical from a pricing perspective, and any subsequent changes to the COO will trigger repricing.

Critical success factors in managing pricing volatility

Now that we have covered how to optimally set prices at the ex-factory level to maximize the commercial opportunity, reimbursement, and formulary inclusion, let's talk about how to manage pricing throughout the life cycle of the product. There are many events after launch that can trigger repricing, which increases market volatility. What are the key events that trigger repricing after launch? Essentially, there are two broad categories: external factors and internal factors.

External factors

- *Market authorization renewal*
- *Mandatory procedures*, such as the price harmonization mandated by the Gulf Cooperation Council (GCC) rules, require regular harmonization.
- *Loss of exclusivity.* This will automatically trigger repricing.
- *Changes in rules and regulations.* Many countries update their pricing governance and rules regularly, so these changes in the pricing rules and governance can trigger repricing.
- *Currency fluctuations.* These can lead to significant price volatility, which will require repricing to support a sustainable pricing system.
- *Market competition.* Although this usually has a direct impact on the net price, not the ex-factory price, it is an important one to keep in mind.

Internal factors

- *Site transfer.* When products are sourced from different countries and if the product is registered from one site, then the product is moved to manufacturing and released at a different site, and this

will trigger repricing.
- *Change in the COO.* This happens in cases where the MA holder changes or because of a change in the product's manufacturing site.
- *Variations or changes in the label.* In certain cases, these will trigger repricing (major, not minor variations).
- *New launches or new indications.* These can trigger repricing; however, currently, MENA countries do not use indication-based pricing in price-setting, and expanded indications do not trigger repricing.
- *Suboptimal pricing strategy.* This will contribute significantly to price volatility, whether it is in tender prices or confidential commercial deals.

How do we best manage these events to minimize price volatility? There are several things that companies can do.

- To whatever extent possible, time any internal price-triggering event with external events. For example, if there is a site change planned and an MA renewal, time the events together. Also, if there will be a loss of exclusivity, which would trigger repricing automatically, and if there are other internal events that can trigger repricing, time events together to minimize the number of times the product will have to go through repricing.
- Wherever possible and helpful, use centralized procedures (or file simultaneously in different countries in the region that reference each other) to minimize the frequency of price-harmonization cycles, particularly in markets like the GCC countries, where if the company registers products at different times, then the renewal cycle will change, which will lead to a continuous cycle of price harmonization.
- Where allowed, use different access solutions such as multi-branding and/or managed entry agreements (MEA) (explained in detail in Chapters 5 and 6) to overcome price volatility.

One of the key challenges in pricing in MENA is the impact of a huge price reduction, which can reach 60 to 70 percent in certain markets and happens at the time of market authorization renewal. The reason for this huge drop is that during the five-year period where the prices in MENA are fixed for the duration of marketing authorization, the prices in the reference countries go through multiple price reductions. The huge price drop may be unsustainable for the company, especially in small markets. The implications of this on the local markets is one of two things:

1. Where the ex-factory price and the net price (market price) in the local market are close to the current ex-factory price, which happens when there are few commercial deals taking place, and most of the product sales are done at the ex-factory price level. In this case, the company may have to either withdraw the product or stop all medical and promotional activities because it will no longer be sustainable to sell the product at the new very low price.

2. Where the net price (market price) in the local market is significantly lower than the ex-factory price, which happens when there are multiple confidential commercial deals in the market. In this case, the new low ex-factory price may be more acceptable to the company (or at least will have a less negative impact on P&L). However, depending on how low the new price is, the company may not support the sustainability of that price level and there may be a risk of product withdrawal.

In some countries where companies move the product to local manufacturing as a mechanism to protect the price—which is the case, for example, in Saudi Arabia, when the product moves into full local manufacturing—there is price protection for five years. That strategy will work in terms of the price-protection mechanism. However, the challenge is when generics become available and there is a loss of exclusivity. In this case, while the difference in the ex-factory price between the original brand and the generic could be 20 percent (as per the current pricing rule), the difference in the net price between the generic (as they may be giving large FOC products to penetrate the market) and the net price of the protected brand under the local manufacturing agreement is huge. Unless the company has sizable private-market sales at the ex-factory price, keeping the ex-factory price high will not be advantageous.

One of the potential ways of dealing with the issue of a huge drop in ex-factory prices that happens at times of MA renewal—although it is controversial—is a voluntary reduction in the ex-factory price. The company can do this strategically somewhere during the five-year marketing-authorization period. This will allow the company to rebase its operation and minimize the impact of the price cliff. Some companies use this approach to make headroom for innovation by negotiating lower ex-factory prices on established products when introducing a new, innovative product. I will cover this in greater detail when we talk about the MEAs later, in Chapter 5. Irrespective of the trigger event for pricing, and whether it is at the ex-factory level or at the net price level, it is very important from a business-planning perspective to incorporate the expected prices in the business-planning cycle during long-range planning.

Before we conclude this chapter, here are some practical dos and don'ts from a pricing perspective.

Dos and don'ts from a pricing perspective

Do ...

- follow the country's pricing rules.
- communicate with health authorities proactively, transparently, and truthfully.
- proactively manage pricing and repricing early on and integrate them into the business-planning cycle.
- proactively manage the ex-factory and net prices in countries with currency fluctuations to minimize the IRP risk.
- proactively manage price-triggering events.
- negotiate, negotiate, and negotiate with authorities.

Don't ...

- start a price war—everyone will lose.
- talk about the price if the stakeholders do not well understand and appreciate the value.
- register a product if you don't intend to launch it. It may sound odd, but it does happen that some companies register a product and never launch it.

- give a low price for a short-term win that will not be sustainable in the long term.
- set the price based on the competitor's price and ignore your product price in the reference-price countries.

Summary

Pricing is one of the most strategic decisions that companies make about their products as it will decide a product's success or failure. Pricing rules in MENA countries are complicated and require a good understanding of the reference-pricing principles and systematic, continuous, and careful monitoring to minimize volatility, which can have a significant impact on the business. Pricing should be a core competency of the MA team. To manage price-setting optimally, the MA team needs to manage price-triggering events carefully, both internally and externally, to ensure sustainability.

4

VALUE AND MARKET ACCESS

In Chapter 1, I mentioned that value means different things to different people. From a health-care perspective, different stakeholders—payers (both public and private), prescribers, health-care professionals, patients, and their caregivers—perceive the value of pharmaceutical innovation differently. This is mainly because different stakeholders have different disease priorities, different levels of access to treatment options, different economic buying power, and different affordability levels.

In this chapter, we will take a closer look at the relationship between the price of medicine and value in the context of the whole health-care system. We will discuss why it's not the price of a pharmaceutical product that matters; it's the value perception.

Let's start with the definition of value. We can define value as "how much a product, good, or service is worth." The economic value is a measure of the benefit provided by a good or service to the recipient of the good or service, usually measured in monetary value (expressed in a different currency). Therefore, when we're talking about the value of a pharmaceutical product, we're saying, "What is the maximum amount of money a payer is willing and able to pay for the product?" Given the diverse payer mix in the MENA region, the payers here could be the governments in countries where a large public sector is the main payer, or it could be private health insurance, or it could be the patients who pay for their health-care out of their own pockets.

From a pharmaceutical-market perspective, new trends are shaping the pricing and value equation. First, there has been an explosion of new therapies in health-care in almost all the therapeutic areas and disease states, and new technologies used in the management of diseases. Therefore, payers are now saying that they are concerned about the high cost of new therapies and emerging technologies in general. They are also worried about not being able to afford everything that might come to them. So, they are getting selective and are only showing interest in new technologies if they are truly innovative and can improve the outcomes for patients. Payers have introduced formal processes for value-based reimbursements and are tracking health outcomes to ensure that products are giving value in real-world settings. In short, they are saying, "We want to focus on value for money." Therefore, there is a shift in the health-care ecosystem from the old world to the new world—see **Figure 11**, which compares the old world (a price-and-cost-based system) and the new world (a value-based system).

As shown in **Figure 11**, high prices for pharmaceuticals and broad access to therapies with few restrictions placed on product use characterized the old world. The system was based on costs and price per pill or price per volume and there was little focus on driving efficiencies in the health-care system. In the new world, it's more of a value-based or outcome-based approach (we will cover this in Chapter 5) where there is a lot of focus on return on investments made in health-care. From value-assessment processes, health-care systems are introducing HTA (health technology assessment). It's more common to have a restricted reimbursement environment, as opposed to an open reimbursement environment. Many countries have introduced "positive lists" or essential drug lists of products, as opposed to open formulary. And they're also introducing new reimbursement measures, such as a tiered co-payment system, where patients bear part of the cost of prescription medicine. Comparative effectiveness is becoming more important to look at the new, innovative therapies in the context of the added value that they bring above and beyond what is already on the market. Lastly, efficiency and sustainability are becoming the new trends.

Figure 11: The evolving health-care ecosystem – the old and the new

Old World
- Higher Prices
- Broader Access
- Fewer restrictions
- Cost-based system
  - "Price per pill"
  - Volume based
  - Tender based
- Ignoring inefficiencies

New World
- Value-based (outcomes-based)
- Focus on ROI
- Health Technology Assessment (HTA)
- Restricted reimbursement
  - Positive List
  - Essential drug list
  - Tiered Co-payment
- Comparative effectiveness
- Efficiency and Sustainability

Why are the prices of pharmaceuticals and drug budgets always a focus?

Simply put, a pharmaceutical budget is always a focus for all stakeholders because of the old saying, "What gets measured gets managed." That's right. The pharmacy budget is always under scrutiny because it's very easy to measure and obtain compared to the other components of the health-care system, such as physician fees, hospitalizations, and diagnostics. But let's put the pharmaceutical budget in perspective. As you can see in **Figure 12**, when we look at the pharmaceutical budget on its own, it always appears as the major standalone "cost." That should not be the case. We should always see it as part of an integrated approach to health-care, where the pharmaceutical budget brings added value to the overall health-care system by way of medical cost offsets and/or disease prevention. Investments made in pharmaceutical spending will have a direct impact on the overall health expenditure where proper use leads to medical-cost offsets, seen by way of reductions in hospitalization and/or other health-care system uses, in addition to improvements in patients' HrQOL. The diffusion of pharmaceutical innovations in the last few decades has helped drive significant improvements in key health indicators (such as life expectancy and improved survival).

As said earlier, in the new world, the focus, when it comes to pharmaceutical spending, is on VBC and return on investment—by society in general, but particularly by the payers. So, let's talk about the value from a health-care perspective. (See also **Figure 13**.)

As defined by Professor Michael Porter from Harvard University, health-care value refers to the patient-health outcomes achieved by each dollar spent. Why is this an important concept to emphasize in health-care? The answer is this: the sustainability of the health-care system should be the key focus from a health-care-spending perspective. A health-care system that is value-based will have the following benefits:

1. Strong patient-centricity and more transparency on patient-outcome measures. The focus is on how we intercede with interventions that bring value to the patient and the health-care system.

2. The focus will be on improvement and efficiency in resource allocation.

Value and Market Access 65

Figure 12: The pharmaceutical budget in perspective

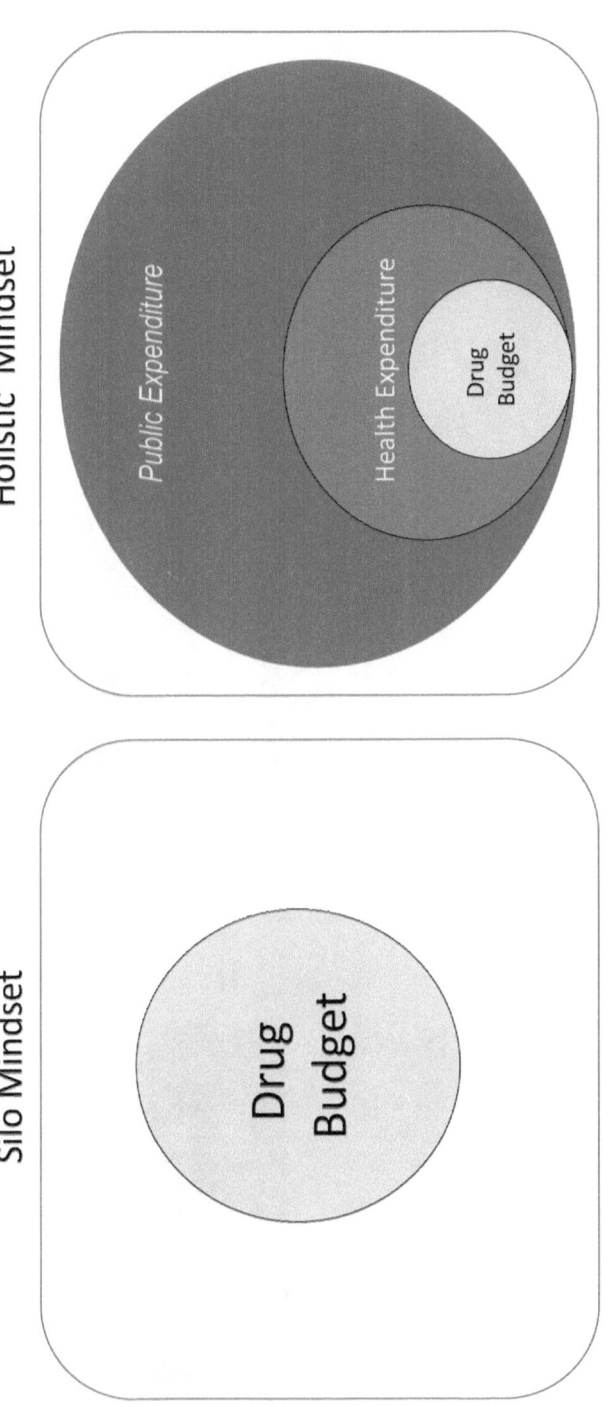

Figure 13: Definition of value in health-care

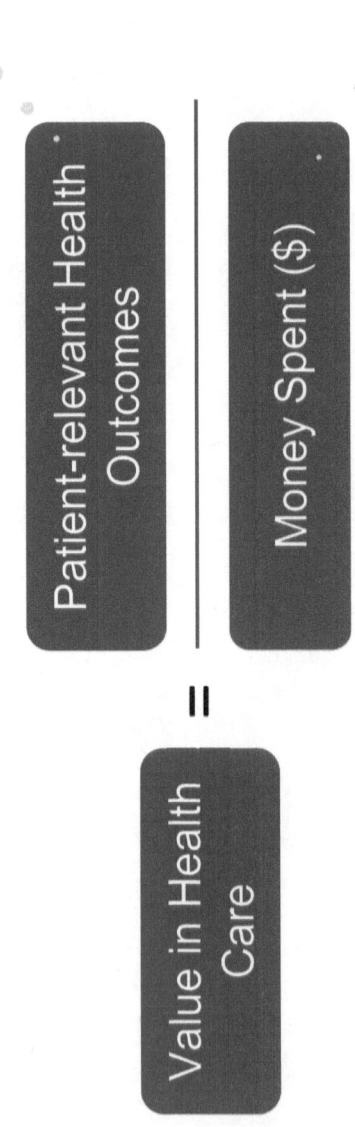

Porter ME. What is value in health care? N Engl J Med 2010; 363:2477-81

3. The focus of research and investment will be on valuable areas that bring added value to the health-care system. Therefore, that system will allow for a continuous stream of innovation and will always embrace innovation that brings value to the overall health-care system.

Value-based pricing

With the evolution of value-based health-care, value-based pricing appeared as a new mechanism for the pricing of pharmaceuticals. VBP in pharmaceuticals is "the use of formal pharmacoeconomic assessment to inform decisions on pricing and/or reimbursement," sometimes also referred to as "the practice of formal assessment of the added therapeutic value of the new product over existing competitors used to determine or negotiate the price." As we discussed in Chapter 3, VBP is a recently introduced mechanism to reward products that bring incremental value to the system. Obviously, this is an important concept that EMs should embrace. However, several practical challenges may limit the implementation of VBP in many emerging markets, including those in the MENA region. There are two aspects to these challenges:

- **Methodological perspective**

    a) There is no accepted definition of *value* agreed upon by all payers.

    b) Which perspective do we take when assessing value—payer perspective, patient perspective, or societal perspective?

    c) What is the right competitor to consider when assessing incremental value? We know that health-care systems use different standards of care—therefore, the competitor in one market may be different from the competitor in another market.

    d) Which incremental value should we focus on when assessing value—clinical, economic, or humanistic improvements?

    e) How do we value the incremental improvement and what threshold can we consider "acceptable value"?

- **Market dynamics and implementation perspective**

    a) As explained in Chapter 3, the registration of ex-factory prices in all MENA countries is based on the IRP rules. Therefore, replacing the IRP-based system with VBP would require major changes to the laws, which must be approved by the legislative bodies in the respective countries. With the challenges listed above, and the lack of technical capabilities in many countries to do formal value-based assessments, it is not practical, at least in the short term, to have VBP as the mechanism replacing the IRP system.

    b) The value of products varies in different countries based on disease incidence and prevalence and availability of different treatment options in the market. For example, Egypt may value a product for hepatitis C far more than Jordan or the UAE does, because Egypt has a higher prevalence of hepatitis C.

    c) Currently, with a few exceptions, there is a universal lack of data on disease prevalence, costs, and outcomes needed to be able to develop country-specific value-based assessments.

What is the significance of this from an MA perspective? Value-based health-care means that the activities of the health sector should be oriented, organized, and funded to maximize health benefits for both payers and society. However, many of the markets in MENA lack universal health coverage where societal value is important and measured. In some ways, countries are currently using some sort of VBP, in the sense that they manage reimbursement and negotiate the price of pharmaceuticals, at least in some circumstances, based on their therapeutic value. To the extent that price registration and reimbursement prices are separate, and there is a mechanism for implementing and keeping confidential net prices, the system can work well, as is the case now in many of the European and other well-developed markets. The problem arises, however, in countries where the registered price is the same as the reimbursement price. In this case, if the VBP can lead to lower prices in the country, based on its socio-economic status and other health-care factors, companies may be willing to accept the price, in line with VBP, but if other countries in the region want to reference the lower VBP and mandate it for their local market, then the situation will be different, and there will be implications:

- Because of the low price mandated by IRP rules, companies may not launch the product (or launch it very late, near the loss of exclusivity timelines).
- Diffusion of innovations will vary greatly between countries in the region, creating inequalities that can become public-health problems.
- If a product is launched in a low-price market in the region, it can lead to cross-border trade (also known as parallel importation), which is associated with many issues from medical and commercial perspectives. Therefore, the critical role of the MA function is (a) to ensure the best price registration, one that mitigates IRP risks; and (b) to ensure there is a mechanism for a confidential net price that allows for the launch of products in low-price markets and markets with affordability challenges.

Value-based reimbursement decisions in MENA

Currently, most MENA countries do not use value-based reimbursement decisions. There is, however, a growing interest in adopting value-based reimbursement through the adaptation of global HTA methods. Some important challenges face companies in implementing value-based reimbursement negotiations, such as:

1. Lack of understanding of the true spirit of VBC and so limiting it to performing cost-effectiveness analysis on a product, which can often result in negotiating prices down or limiting reimbursement and formulary listing.
2. Lack of technical expertise among the reimbursement authorities to do the assessment, even if a value-based dossier is submitted (many companies in the region also lack the expertise to develop value-based dossiers).
3. Lack of data specifically on epidemiology, health-care resource use, and costs that would allow companies to submit country-specific economic evaluations as part of value-based reimbursement negotiations.

4. In some countries, there are competing and conflicting priorities between different agencies or reimbursement decision-makers in the same country. This happens where there are different purchasing authorities and each one has its formulary and reimbursement process. One purchasing authority may want to negotiate a price based on VBP and the other to negotiate based on the lowest price. There is also the situation where the main goal of the negotiating person is to secure a lower price to show their managers that they secured a lower price than the one originally proposed by the company because, from their perspective, this is what is important to them (what a win looks like to them).

One of the critical points to consider in this regard is the transferability of the HTA decision from one country to another, which is, unfortunately, being done in many markets where they look to the HTA agencies that are prominent in the world, such as the National Institute for Health and Care Excellence (NICE) in the United Kingdom, or the Scottish Medicines Consortium (SMC), or the Pharmaceutical Benefits Advisory Committee (PBAC) in Australia, or the Canadian Agency for Drugs and Technologies in Health (CADTH). Some of the reimbursement authorities in MENA look at the decisions made by these HTA bodies in the above countries and they try to apply these decisions on pricing and reimbursement locally, without considering the disparate health-care systems' setup, financing, and values. The problems with this approach are:

- These HTA agencies conduct their assessment from their own country's perspective, which has its standards for clinical care, including choice of products and competitors, health-care resource-use patterns, and costs.
- It makes transferability of the results to other countries inapplicable because of the differences in clinical practice patterns, different cost structures, and different health-care-system values. MENA countries that adapt reimbursement decisions by these international organizations will not yield the same results as those yielded for the original country where the HTA agency

performed the analysis from their perspective.
- Since the HTA often makes reimbursement decisions after price negotiations between companies and the countries, the net price negotiated by these prominent HTA bodies is confidential, making the transfer of the finding less applicable to other countries. The confidential net price between companies and governments is actually to the benefit of the countries; otherwise, the diffusion of innovation will be diminished significantly.

Therefore, given the importance of VBC to the sustainability and future of the health-care system, it is important to shape policies in this area. The consequences of failure to shape policy in the market could be dire. First, the sustainability of the health-care system will be put at risk. Second, a significant delay in the introduction of innovative products to the market can occur. Third, from a company perspective, the launch of products without full articulation of value perception will lead to lower prices, which can delay or prevent the launch of innovative, life-saving therapies. Fourth, it can also lead to non-reimbursement or significant restriction on reimbursement, which will, in turn, lead to slower product uptake and/or lead to significant price erosion.

Policy shaping to enable access

Market shaping is a critical success factor when launching a new product, particularly biological or high-value products where the prices are very high. Launching without shaping the environment to ensure that all stakeholders understand and appreciate the value of the new product will be detrimental because it will put at risk the commercial success of the product.

Policy shaping is a critical part of MA activities. It requires an integrated approach, focusing on the following four key areas:

1. policies and procedures in health-care that govern the practices of the health-care system
2. an integrated care model that considers the whole system, not silos
3. outcome measures that focus on performance and what matters to patients and payers

4. the prevailing health-care payment system in the country.

Figure 14 gives a more detailed description of each of these areas.

Key activities to promote value-based care

Given the importance of value-based care to building a sustainable health-care system, what can the MA teams do to promote VBC? They can:

- educate policymakers on the worth of VBC and why it is in their best interests to focus on it. This can be done by:

    a) promoting evidence-based medicine (EBM), which allows for an integrated approach to health-care costs not focused on pharmaceuticals alone

    b) advocating for outcomes-based agreements, which drive efficiency in the system

    c) generating high-quality data to promote EBM and VBC in decision-making, including cost-effectiveness analyses, comparative selectiveness research, and RWE

- continue to invest in generating real-world evidence to inform policy decisions and communicate findings to decision-makers
- collaborate with stakeholders to develop and promote relevant and transparent key performance indicators to use in the decision-making process
- engage with stakeholders—the MA function should engage payers, providers, professional societies, and patients to ensure they fully appreciate and understand VBC and its relevance to each of them.

Summary

Focusing on VBC is critical to building a sustainable health-care system. Many countries are moving toward the VBC model. However, there is still a lot of room for improvement in many aspects that countries and the private sector need to collaborate on. Companies should collaborate with all stakeholders to shape the health-care environment. While focusing on VBC, it's also important to address the rising pharmaceutical

Figure 14: Approach to policy shaping activities to promote value-based care
Enablers of VBC

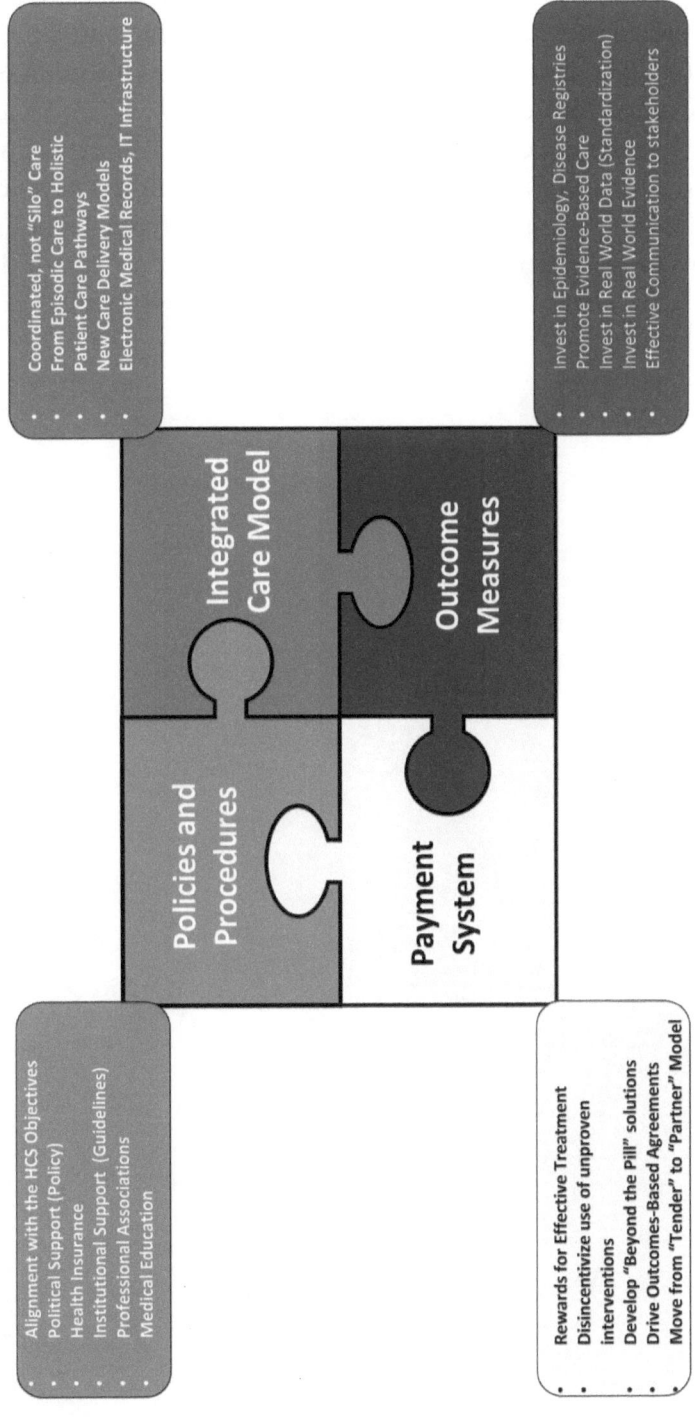

budget and put it in the right perspective. In this regard, addressing the continued increase in the health-care budget, including the pharmaceutical budget, is critical to ensuring the continued diffusion of health-care innovation to the EMs.

In the next chapter, we will focus on the importance of developing proven, practical, and innovative solutions to address payer concerns and challenges. These solutions apply to all payer types, including OOP patients in self-pay markets.

5

DELIVERING WINNING MARKET ACCESS SOLUTIONS

Before we talk about winning market access solutions to address payer concerns, let's talk briefly about some of the unique situations when it comes to pharmaceutical reimbursement in MENA markets. One of the distinctive things about the MENA region is that it has countries with the highest and the lowest GDP per capita in the world and one of the lowest health expenditures per capita in the world. There are no national reimbursement systems or universal health coverage in most of the countries; brand loyalty is very high; and, from a patient perspective, there is a high expectation of prompt access to global pharmaceutical brands at the lowest possible price.

There are six important questions related to this unique situation:

1. Do patients in each country have good access to health-care in general?
2. Is the product (brand) available in the local markets?
3. Does the product offer good value for money at the respective prices in local markets?
4. Is it accessible to all eligible patients?

5. Is it affordable?
6. Is paying for it sustainable?

The ability to answer these key questions is what makes the MA role so critical in the pharmaceutical industry.

So, what is the market access role within an organization?

The MA role is threefold: to develop strategies and generate evidence that supports the product's value proposition, to deliver customizable solutions that achieve early access, and to maintain optimal reimbursement of products to improve patient outcomes. To do all this, the MA team needs to know and understand the customer's operating business model to develop the right access solutions. This is where the customizable approach to delivering access solutions becomes a critical success factor. Companies often use MEAs (managed entry agreements, sometimes also referred to as special access schemes) to achieve this critical success factor.

What is a managed entry agreement?

As defined by Dr. Maryanne Klemp and colleagues in a 2011 article in the *International Journal of Technology Assessment in Healthcare*, a managed entry agreement is "an arrangement between a manufacturer and a payer/provider that enables access to (coverage/reimbursement of) a health technology, subject to specified conditions. These arrangements can use various mechanisms to address uncertainty about the performance of technologies or to manage the adoption of technologies, to maximize their use or limit their budget impact."[2] In the literature, you will often find different terms used to describe these MEAs. Some of the most common terms are innovative pricing models, risk-sharing agreements, value-based pricing, pay-for-performance agreements, patient access schemes, and managed entry schemes. In the next section, we will detail the patient access schemes and their use in the MENA region as a common access strategy.

---

2   Marianne Klemp, Katrine B Frønsdal, and Karen Facey, "What Principles Should Govern the Use of Managed Entry Agreements?" *International Journal of Technology Assessment in Healthcare*, 2011, vol. 27, no. 1, pages 77–83.

As illustrated in **Figure 15**, the access scheme is based on the three different levers that health-care can use to ensure access to innovative therapies: *price, value,* and *volume*. Broadly speaking, the approach to the access solution is based on two distinct approaches. The first is a volume-based approach, one widely used in the marketplace for decades. The second approach is a value-based approach, which is a new trend appearing in many countries. Additionally, there are other types of access programs that can support both the value-based schemes and the volume-based approaches, and I will describe these in the next section.

Volume-based schemes

There are four types of volume-based schemes:

1. **Volume-based solutions**

    a) *A price-volume agreement*, which essentially offers lower prices on predefined volume thresholds agreed between the company and the payer (for the purchase of goods or services). As an example, for a product with an ex-factory price of 50 USD, if a payer buys 100,000 units, the net price to the payer reduces to 45 USD. If the payer buys 500,000 units, the net price reduces to 40 USD. And if the payer buys 1,000,000 units or above, then the price reduces to 35 USD. Two important considerations here: (1) the company and the payer usually keep the net price confidential; (2) to reach the net price agreed on between the company and the payer, the company may give FOC goods to protect the price.

    b) In a *price-volume discount*, companies often offer variable discounts on predefined quantities. For example, a company may propose that if a payer buys 100,000 units of a particular product, the customer will get a 5 percent discount off the ex-factory price. If the payer buys 200,000 units, the discount will increase to 7 percent, and if the payer buys 500,000, the discount will increase to 10 percent off the ex-factory price. Here, it's important to note that, where allowed, a company sometimes uses a rebate instead of a straight discount, which means that the company will wait until the payer buys the predefined volume before it applies the agreed discount.

Figure 15: Patient Access Schemes
Delivering value through customized access solutions

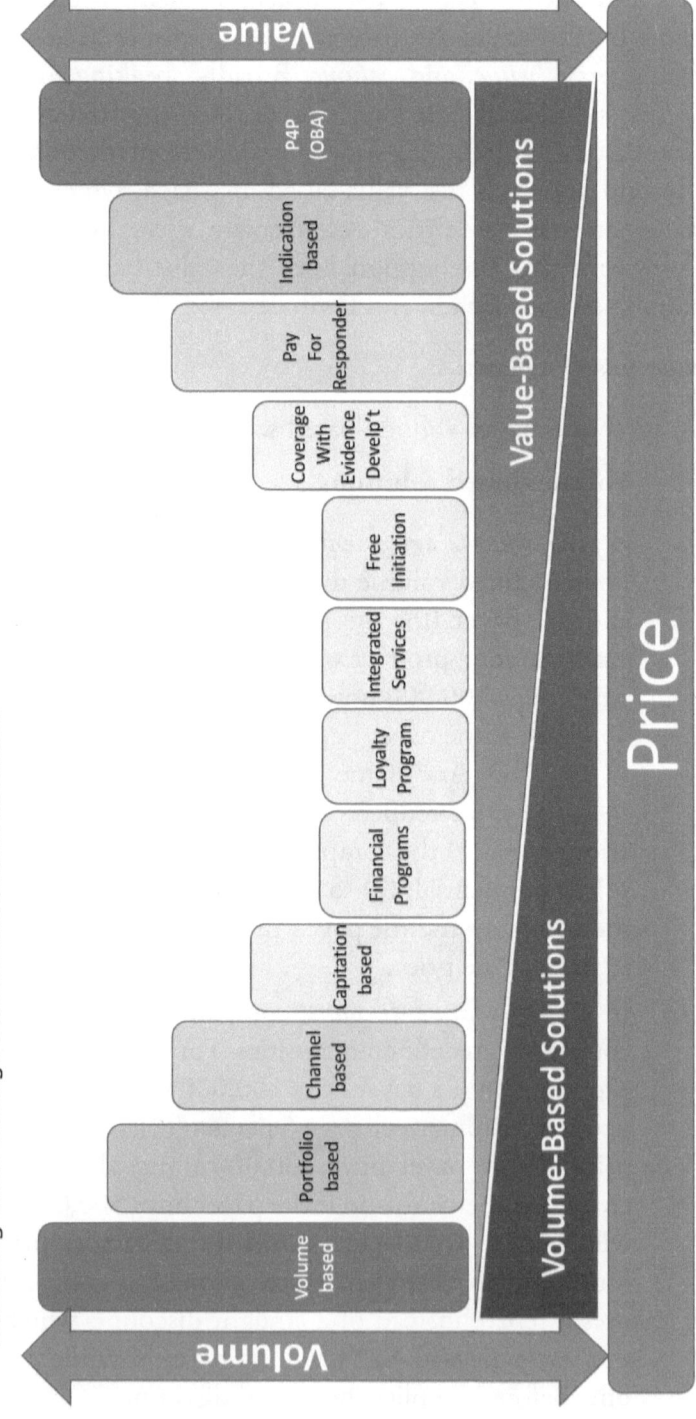

3. **Portfolio-based solutions**

The portfolio-based schemes can be one of two options:

a) The first option is *portfolio trade-off*, where a company may trade-off the prices of old products to secure access to innovative products at the best prices for both parties. Companies can give the trade-off as a straight discount on the ex-factory price of older products or give another form of discount such as FOC.

b) The second type of portfolio-based scheme is the *portfolio bundle*. In this scheme, the company could give one price for a predefined portfolio of products, commonly in the same disease area. For example, a company may offer portfolio products used to manage patients with cardiovascular diseases (e.g., a statin and a beta-blocker or angiotensin-converting enzyme inhibitor) at one fixed price. A second example is if a company has products that treat a disease state as first-line, second-line, or third-line therapy, the company could offer one price per patient to manage all lines of therapy. The third example would be discounted prices on multiple products bought together (e.g., if a company has product A, product B, and product C, and the payer is buying all three products, the company can give discounted prices on all three), if and only if the payer buys all three together.

3. **Channel-based solutions**

In this scheme, a company may offer a price for a particular channel (MOH, Social Security Department, Private Health Insurance Network, etc.), assuming the channel is a "closed system," with no product spillover to other market segments within the country. In this case, depending on the size of the channel, the company may decide to have separate product packaging to prevent spillover and product diversion, or it could make special arrangements to have channel marking on the outer package itself (where needed, the company must of course secure preclearance from the MOH).

4. **Capitation-based solutions.** In a capitation-based scheme, the company caps the price either on a per-patient per-year basis or at a predefined population and volume. For example, a company may offer one price for cancer treatment on an annual basis for every patient that uses their product, irrespective of the number of doses or combination of different dose strengths of the product. Or the company may offer to cap the maximum budget the payer will pay to manage a predefined patient population based on well-established utilization patterns and defined daily dose per patient per year. Both parties will agree on a volume that can cover the patients' needs for a year, and they will cap the total budget each payer will pay. Should the volume increase for the same specified number of patients, the company will supply the extra volumes at no cost to the payer. As an example, let's say that a company agrees with a payer that if a customer has 100,000 patients with an average expected use of six units per patient per year, then the expected total volume is 600,000 units per year. If the usage pattern changes—for example, every patient ends up using eight units instead of six—then the company essentially will bear the cost of the two incremental units per patient for the whole year and bear the cost of the additional 200,000 units that were consumed by the patients in this account.

Value-based schemes

There are four different value-based schemes:

1. **Coverage with evidence development**

   The payer agrees to reimburse for the new treatment or add it to their formulary while the company agrees to collect more evidence prospectively, usually in the form of an RWE to address the payer concerns about the new product, whether they be around the uncertainty of the benefit of the product in a real-world setting, or the maximum use per patient, or other concerns. In this scheme, the payer will pay the full price submitted by the company (or a negotiated price) if the evidence generated supports the value of the product based on the endpoints agreed to between the company and the payer. If the evidence does not support value, then the company will refund the payer the part of the drug budget spent on the product.

2. **Pay for responder**

In this scheme, the payer pays only for patients who respond to the treatment. If the patient does not respond, the company does not charge for its product. This is commonly done with high-value products, where a companion diagnostic is not available to find responders for the new treatment. The company allows the payer to pay only for patients who respond and remain on treatment (usually at the full price requested by the company). With this scheme, the company takes all the risk on any patient who does not respond to therapy as a way of maximizing the payer investment in the new product.

3. **Indication-based scheme (also known as price-by-indication)**

In this scheme, the company negotiates different prices with the payer for the same product in the different indications for which the product is approved. This obviously applies to a product with multiple indications. The underlying assumption, in this case, is: (1) the first approved indication would have the highest price that the product will be registered at with the health authorities, or (2) the country has a mechanism for registering (or reimbursing) a higher price based on the value of the new indication. From a MENA perspective, this scheme is not commonly used because, in many of the accounts, it's difficult to track product use by indication, or it's not possible to get a higher price from the initially registered price. However, with greater investments in electronic health records and digital health, or to the extent that a payer can track use by indications, companies can negotiate different reimbursement prices (net prices) for the different indications, which could be a practical solution, at least in some MENA countries.

4. **Pay-for-performance (also known as OBAs)**

This is a type of risk-share agreement (RSA) where the company removes uncertainty around whether the product will perform in the real world as it did in the controlled clinical trial setting. In this type of scheme, the company and a payer make an agreement whereby the payer pays the negotiated price when the mutually agreed outcome is achieved in the target population. If the outcome is not achieved or achieved below the pre-specified threshold, the payer pays a lower price. This is the most complicated and time-consuming scheme as it involves a careful design, prospective data collection, and tracking. The outcome is usually a key endpoint specified in the product label based on the results from the pivotal studies of the product (e.g., hospitalization, relapse event, progression-free survival).

Now that we've covered the volume-based scheme and the value-based scheme, let's move on to those access schemes that can run as standalone access solutions, or in combination with the previously discussed volume-based and/or value-based schemes.

There are four common types of schemes:

1. **Financial programs**

   There are two types: (a) *Special financing scheme.* For patients who pay for medicine themselves and cannot afford to pay the full payment of the product at once, the company may work with a third party (banks, credit-card companies, etc.) to put a payment program in place over time and the company may cover the cost of financing the payment over time. So, the patient essentially makes smaller installments of the total cost of the product rather than pays the full amount at once. (b) *Co-payment coverage.* This applies to situations where the patient pays a co-payment (a fixed amount or percentage of the actual cost of the product) as part of the reimbursement of the product. In this case, the company agrees to cover, partially or fully, the co-payment amount borne by the patient as a way of minimizing the financial burden on the patient.

2. **Loyalty programs**

   The company agrees to pay or reward patients for their continued use of their product by offering the product as FOC goods for a predefined number of treatment cycles. For example, if the patient is on therapy for a full year, the company may reward the patient with two months free of charge to keep the patient on therapy.

3. **Integrated services (also known as value-add services)**

The company undertakes to cover the cost of services related to a particular service or requirement associated with the use of their product. For example, if a product requires a particular test before treatment initiation, or observation after the first dose, or prophylactic use of a product before treatment initiation, the company will commit to cover the cost of the requirement as a way of minimizing the overall cost of treatment on the payer and to minimize any potential disadvantage versus competitors' products.

4. **Free treatment initiation**

In this program, the company agrees to supply treatment initiation as FOC goods (or discounted price) for their product. This is mostly used in cases with products that require loading doses upon treatment initiation—for example, a product that is intended for administration as a monthly dose but requires weekly administration for the first month. The payer (or a self-pay patient) may not be able to afford the cost of four doses the first month. So, the company may decide to give the first three doses of the first month as FOC, and the payer pays the monthly cost onward (maintenance cost). Please note, in this example, it is also possible that companies may combine the capitation program with the free initiation as a package to address the high cost of initiation for the product.

In all the above schemes, the MA team must work with the compliance team and the legal team to ensure that any access scheme proposed by the company does not violate any local rules (written or implied) before embarking on any initiative. Equally important is the need for an exit strategy or clause in any contractual access agreement, whether it is with the government, a private payer, or a self-pay patient.

Use of managed entry agreements in MENA

Many of these MEA schemes have only recently come to the MENA region, although Europe, the United States, and other advanced pharmaceutical markets use them extensively. One research paper, published in 2018 by Christiane Maskineh and Soumana Nasser, has investigated the use of MEAs in the MENA region.[3] The authors surveyed public and private sector decision-makers in select MENA countries to ascertain the extent to which these MEAs were being used to facilitate or improve access to innovative therapies. The study showed that out of the 44 participants who responded to the survey, only 42 percent reported having an MEA running in their institution. Most respondents indicated that the type of scheme most commonly used was the financial-based scheme (price discount treatment or price-volume agreement). This point is important because value-based agreements are generating a lot of interest from payers, but few are being put in place. So, interest may not translate into implementation for several reasons, including the one pointed out above—that the OBA is more complicated and requires far more data (data that may not be easily accessible or not exist) to put together an agreement. Therefore, in many of the MENA countries, the more advanced value-based agreement is currently limited. However, in the future, with a greater focus on VBC, performance indicators, greater use of digital technology, and electronic health records, many countries are likely to use value-based agreements more.

With MENA countries having had limited experience with this type of agreement, it is important to discuss some of the early learnings from global experience, learnings that can be useful as the MA team prepares to use MEAs more in the future. These learnings are:

1. There is almost a universal, genuine interest in many of the countries to use OBAs. However, the interest may not translate into actual adoption and willingness to implement and drive these MEAs in the local setting. And that's because, in some cases, the financial system in the account or the country may not support implementing an OBA, or there are difficulties around getting data that would allow the implementation of an OBA.

2. OBA contracts are far more complicated than the regular contracts that companies and payers are accustomed to drafting.

---

3   Christiane Maskineh and Soumana Nasser, "Managed Entry Agreements for Pharmaceutical Products in Middle East and North African Countries: Payer and Manufacturer Experience and Outlook." *Value in Health Regional Issues* 2019:16C:33–38.

When you want to implement an OBA for the first time, there needs to be patience and persistence in bringing onboard all relevant stakeholders if you want to overcome the obstacles that will inevitably arise along the way.

3. You may want to start the first one in a small account or forward-thinking payer who is keenly interested in driving OBAs locally. Once you do the first one and you know how to do it, then it becomes easier to replicate and scale up to larger institutions.

Stakeholder mapping

Now that we have covered patient access schemes and the different types of MEA used, it's important to talk about stakeholder mapping, because these schemes work differently and are more applicable to certain payer types or accounts than others. An important first step is to be able to do account mapping and know how you will use the different access solutions for the same product to secure formulary listing or reimbursement in the different accounts, even within the same country.

As illustrated in **Figure 16**, it is important before developing the MA strategy that the company maps the key accounts that make up most of the business. It can apply the 80:20 rule here, whereby, if there are too many small payers or accounts, the company focuses on the 20 percent of the accounts that make up 80 to 90 percent of the business. As illustrated in **Figure 16**, the company can map the list of key accounts in the country in terms of their market size, size of the business, their influence level (at the national or regional level, and with other accounts), and how strong the company's relationship is with the respective accounts.

The next step is to name each key account's objectives, business model, and what the main challenges are in the respective disease area (and what the overall challenge is) so you can propose the right access solution for them. Once the account mapping is complete (external assessment), the next step is to do an internal assessment. Essentially, in this step, the most important thing to do is to show the company's long-term goals for the account (from access and reimbursement perspectives) and the key reimbursement challenges the company is facing in each account.

Figure 16: Approach to stakeholders mapping for market access
Detailed mapping of key accounts

Account Name	Market Size (% of Country)	Market Size (% of company's Business)	National Influence 1 (low) → 5 (high)	Company Relationship Strong – moderate – weak
Account Name 1	10%	10%	5	Medium
Account Name 2	20%	10%	2	Weak
Account Name 3	30%	35%	3	Moderate
Account Name 4	40%	45%	4	Strong

Account Name	Account Objectives	Account Challenge	Company Objectives	Company Challenge (in the account)
Account Name 1	Move into HTA	Reduced drug budget	Remove restrictions	Need stronger advocacy
Account Name 2	Formulary restriction		Formulary listing	Pricing
Account Name 3	Generate local RWE	Significant off-label use	Grow the business	Weak advocacy
Account Name 4	Use CEA to drive Reimbursement	Increase in Biologics use	Maintain leadership	Competitor's price approach

Access solution should be designed to align the company's objectives with the customer's priorities

After completion of the stakeholder mapping, it is important to match the company's objectives with the objectives of each account to negotiate a win-win situation and secure reimbursement, as shown in **Figure 17**. You should do this exercise for every brand the company wants to introduce to the market. It will be the strategic map that lays out the reimbursement and access strategy for the product and you should use it as a guide in the execution plan. For new launches, it is critical that after aligning the launch sequence and the access strategy early on for every product, it is communicated to the cross-functional teams working on the launch of the products.

Summary

1. The first and most important rule to remember is "If it's not broke, don't fix it." The access solutions proposed should be fit-for-purpose and the goal should be to overcome any payer challenges.
2. Know what the real pain point is for the payer and work with the payer to solve it. Do not propose a solution because you've done it with other payers, because each payer is different and has different needs.
3. RSA is maybe the new trend but it's not for everyone. Be pragmatic, and if you propose RSA as an access solution, ensure that it is the right approach, and that the payer has the buy-in and ability to implement it.
4. A value-based solution may not necessarily hasten access. Indeed, because they are more complicated, in some cases they can slow down or delay access.
5. If you're not sure the customer is ready to accept innovative access solutions, don't force it. Shape the market environment first before you propose the solution. If the customer is not ready to embrace a new business model, they're not going to adopt it.
6. Cross-functional alignment on the access strategy early on is critical. Before any pricing discussions, the team should clearly articulate to payers the value.

88 Frontiers in Market Access

Figure 17: Summary of product access strategy by account/customer

	Volume-based	Portfolio-based	Channel-based	Capitation-based	CED	P4 Response	Indication-based	P4P (OBA)	Affordability Programs	Free initiation	Loyalty Program	Integrate service
Account #1								x		x		
Account #2	x			x								
Account #3												
Account #4						x						x

Key Considerations
- Ideally, this should be done before launch
- Should be updated throughout product lifecycle
- Approach and execution must be aligned between Market Access, Commercial, and Medical Affairs.
- Pricing assumptions, solution type and details must be endorsed locally and by the Global Project Team
- Financials must be endorsed by management locally first and then by Regional or Global

6
NEW EVOLVING ACCESS MODELS

In Chapter 5, we discussed the most common trends in access used to address payer challenges. We delved deeper into the use of different types of MEAs (managed entry agreements) to overcome payer challenges. In this chapter, we will focus on two new approaches you can use to expand access, especially—but not exclusively—in self-pay markets where patient affordability is the key challenge. The first approach is PAP (patient affordability programs) and the second is the alternative branding strategy, more commonly referred to as access brand (AB) strategy. We will focus especially on key strategic considerations and operational aspects that the company needs to consider for the sustainability and success of both approaches. We will discuss important company governance and policies that should guide these access solutions and discuss the external issues to consider before the company can embark on this journey.

The affordability pyramid

Let's begin by understanding the so-called affordability pyramid concerning patient access. **Figure 18** outlines three income levels and these are important to keep in mind when adopting a market access perspective:

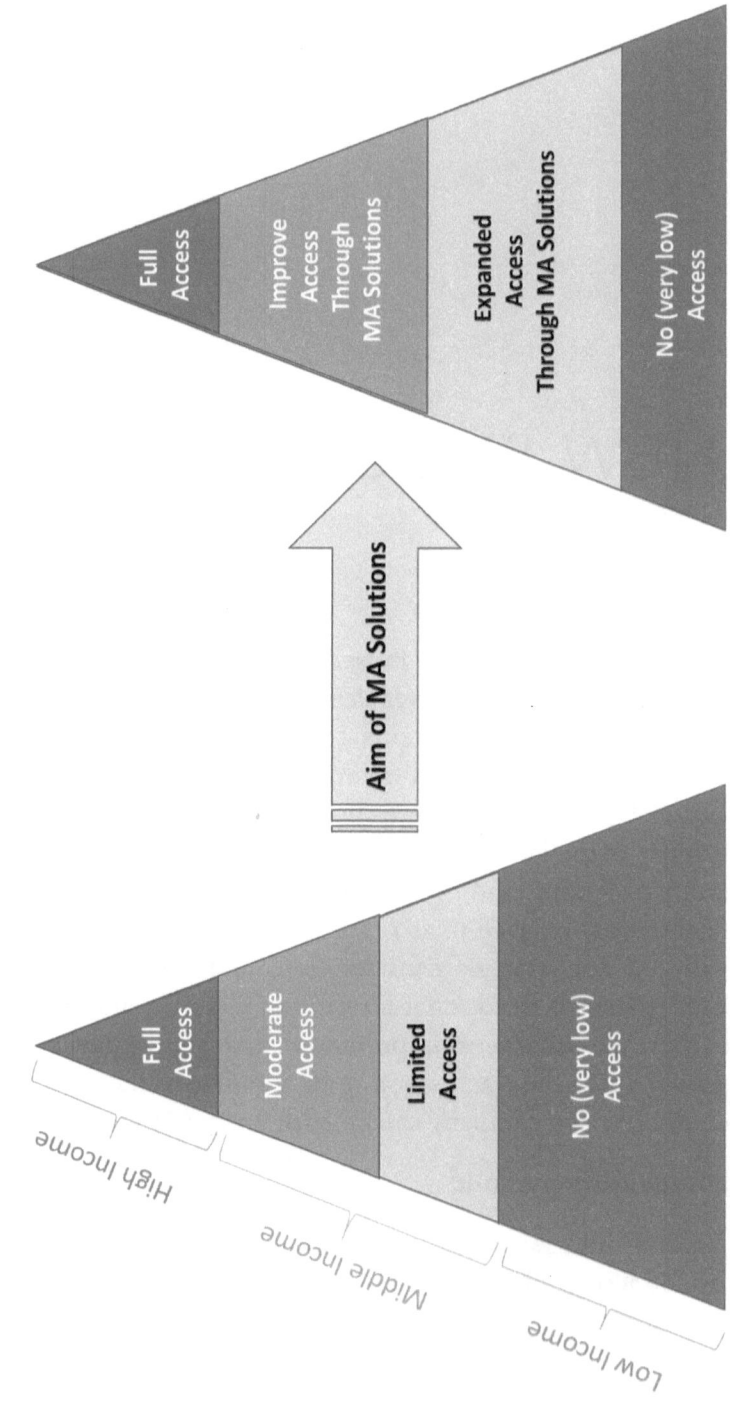

Figure 18: Affordability pyramid and goal of market access

1. The *high-income* level, which is the tip of the pyramid and stands for the smallest part of the pyramid in many countries. Historically, this is where the companies operate when they introduce innovative brands, particularly in low- and middle-income countries (usually private market, select government programs, and/or self-pay).
2. The *middle-income* level, which in some countries is a sizable segment. In other countries, the middle-income level is shrinking and there is more widening of the low-income level.
3. The *low-income* level in many countries of the EM is large, if not the largest segment. This is where access to innovative medicine becomes a challenge in the country.

From an access-to-pharmaceuticals perspective, the three income levels correspond to four different access levels. First, full access at the tip of the pyramid is where people enjoy full access to medicine by having good health insurance coverage. Second is moderate access, wherein patients have good access but not at the same level as full access (it could have some limitations or restrictions). Third is limited coverage (the so-called under-insured) wherein patients have access but with significant restrictions or could also be patients who pay OOP but obviously with significant affordability issues, especially with high-value medicines. The fourth level is "no access," which is at the base of the pyramid (or very limited) where patients may not have access to therapy, or they will have very low access to health-care in general. If they have low access to health-care, by default they will have low or no access to innovative medicine. Given the markedly different access levels, the goal of MA is to expand access and drive it toward the base of the pyramid by using the different access schemes that we discussed in Chapter 5 and will detail in this chapter. It is important to note here that pharmaceutical companies can only reach the very bottom of the pyramid through the philanthropic initiatives that they have in place, especially in low-income countries, and not through traditional access initiatives.

What is a patient affordability program?

Patient affordability programs (PAPs) are access programs put in place by pharmaceutical companies in markets where patients cannot afford innovative medicine. The two main groups of patients this applies to are those who pay for their health-care and hence often cannot afford to pay for pharmaceuticals and those who have some insurance but fall under the category of under-insured.

As you can see in **Figure 19**, there are two common types of PAPs. The first is *individual patient assessment* and the second is the *pre-set (fixed) scheme*.

In the *individual patient assessment* scheme, a company usually hires a third-party company (TPC) to do individual patient assessments to decide their affordability levels. Once the TPC does the affordability-level assessment of individual patients, it puts in place patient-specific access solutions based on a cost-sharing concept, whereby the patient agrees to pay some months based on their income level. Then the pharmaceutical company either provides the rest of the treatment as FOC goods (two-way cost-share model), or the TPC may be able to secure an NGO (a non-government organization) or other funding support to pay for part of the treatment costs (three-way cost-share model). In the two-way cost-share model, the patient agrees to pay, for example, for six months out of the twelve-month annual treatment, and the company pays the remaining six months. In the three-way cost-share model, for example, the patient may be able to pay for five months, the NGO will pay for two months, and therefore the company will pay for the remaining five months out of a twelve-month treatment.

From an operational standpoint, in the individual patient assessment scheme, the cost to set up the program by the TPC can be expensive, especially if the TPC does not have the right infrastructure in the country. The running cost can also be relatively high because of the continual assessment of individual patients. It's also important to note that this scheme is more applicable to specialty products or high-value products, not mass-marketed products. Then, depending on the country, the TPC may manage the distribution of products or it may coordinate directly with the pharmacies or the distributors to ensure delivery of the products once the patient is deemed eligible to take part in the program.

The second type is the *pre-set scheme (fixed)*. In this scheme, the company makes no individualized patient assessment. Instead, it agrees with either the government (if the government of the country is involved) or with an OOP patient. The company agrees on a fixed scheme whereby

Figure 19: Types of patient affordability programs

Individual Patient Assessment Scheme	Fixed, Pre-set Scheme

• Individualized patient assessment, usually by Third Party, to determine affordability level.
• Based on cost-sharing concept where the patient pays certain number of months (or doses) and the company pays the rest. In certain countries, charity and/or NGO may also be part where they donate certain number of doses.
• Can be expensive to set up and maintain.
• More applicable to specialty products, not mass marketed products.
• Depending on the country, Third Party may be responsible for distribution of products, or they coordinate directly with Pharmacies or Distributors.
	• No individualized patient assessment is done.
	• Designed as fixed scheme given as either:
	  • Free of Charge (FOC) goods given (1+1, or 1+2, or 2+3) with every purchase, or
	  • Straight discount applied to the price of the product.
	• Usually done in countries (or accounts) where individual assessment is not feasible, or in case of mass marketed products but with proper distribution channel and where product diversion can be properly prevented.

goods are provided freely. So, the fixed scheme could be that for every unit that the patient buys, they get one unit free, or for every two units they buy, they get one unit free, and so on. It can also be that a straight discount is applied to the price of the product in this scheme. Again, this scheme is usually done in accounts or countries where individual patient assessment either cannot be done or is not feasible or in cases where the product is mass-marketed and where, from a cost perspective, it would be prohibitive to do individual assessments on large patient populations because the cost of running the program could surpass the cost of the product itself in the long run.

Why are these two programs important? One reason is that PAP is one of the main strategies that companies use now to broaden access to innovative medicine, especially since health-care costs in some countries are shifting toward patients. Also, many of the innovative medicines that companies are now launching, especially cancer medicine and biologics (high-value medicine), are very expensive. Therefore, in countries where the patient pays OOP, affordability becomes a key hurdle; without these PAPs, access to the products will be severely restricted or the product may not be launched at all, which means that a large segment of the eligible patient population will be under-served.

It's also important to note that, from a sustainability standpoint, if these PAPs are poorly designed—whether it is a fixed scheme or the individual assessment scheme—or poorly executed, they may only reach a small percentage of the population, which may not be sustainable. Therefore, it's critical to design a PAP carefully to ensure broad access. The PAP should drive access toward the base of the affordability pyramid and not keep it at the tip or in the middle.

Critical success factors for patient-affordability programs

As illustrated in **Figure 20**, there are several critical elements to the design of these affordability programs. You need to have:

- a thorough understanding of the income thresholds in the affordability pyramid—this means having correct data on the different income levels within each category, especially at the middle and base of the pyramid (middle income and low income)

Figure 20: Patient affordability programs design elements

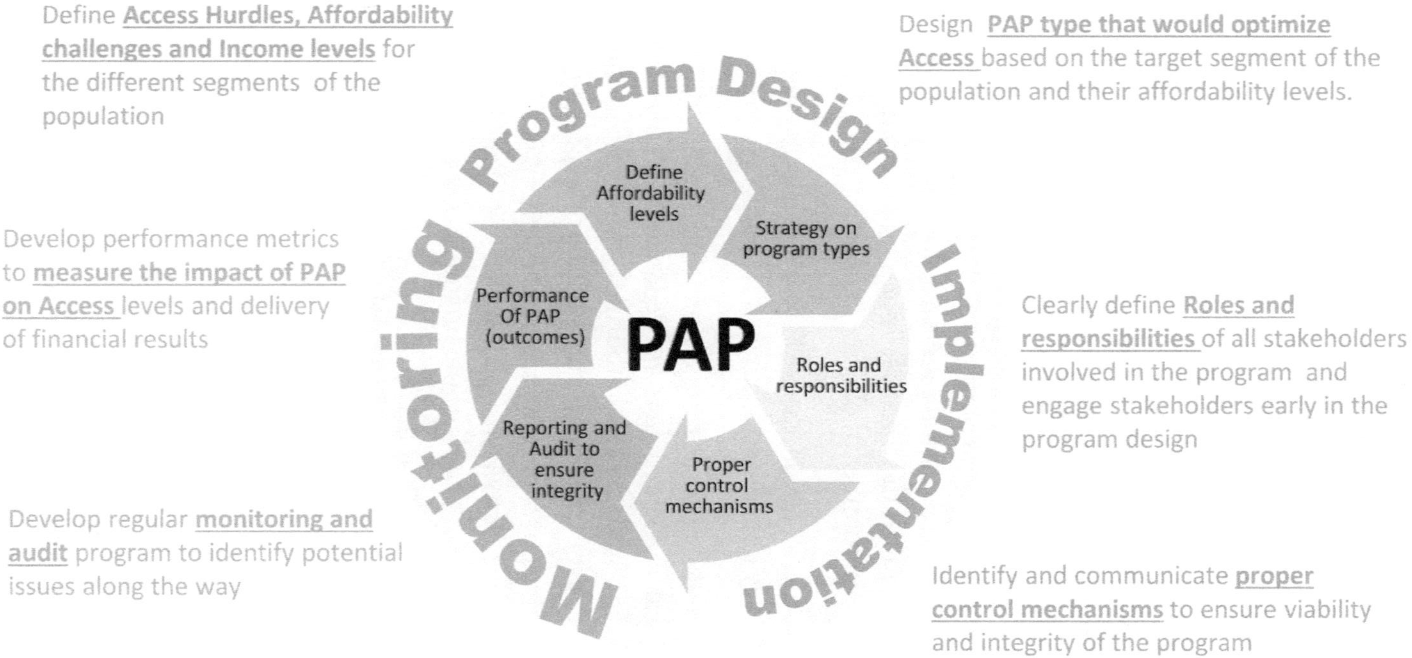

Define **Access Hurdles, Affordability challenges and Income levels** for the different segments of the population

Develop performance metrics to **measure the impact of PAP on Access** levels and delivery of financial results

Develop regular **monitoring and audit** program to identify potential issues along the way

Design **PAP type that would optimize Access** based on the target segment of the population and their affordability levels.

Clearly define **Roles and responsibilities** of all stakeholders involved in the program and engage stakeholders early in the program design

Identify and communicate **proper control mechanisms** to ensure viability and integrity of the program

PAP

Program Design / Implementation / Monitoring

- Strategy on program types
- Roles and responsibilities
- Proper control mechanisms
- Reporting and Audit to ensure integrity
- Performance Of PAP (outcomes)
- Define Affordability levels

- a clear strategy on which segment of the pyramid will be the target of the PAP—you may use different strategies in different segments of the pyramid
- a design that ensures long-term sustainability—to expand access sustainably, it is important to design a PAP carefully because premature termination risks reputational damage
- proper control mechanisms to ensure the integrity of the PAP, prevent any potential misuse, abuse, or potential product diversion—it's equally important to make sure the control mechanism is enforceable in the local settings where you will implement the program
- a proactive, ongoing monitoring system with proper audits to ensure the viability, sustainability, and integrity of the program and adjust the threshold levels, if needed, to ensure that the maximum number of eligible patients benefit.

As you embark on the PAP journey, it's also important to keep in mind the key operational elements, which are:

1. Seek approval from the relevant health authorities in the local markets, where needed, and formally document program approvals by the authorities, showing the conditions attached and/or timelines before you start the program.
2. Have a communication mechanism for all stakeholders (patients, physicians, pharmacies, distributors, and governments) on the elements of the program: objectives, expected outcomes, and monitoring.
3. Make sure you stipulate the patient eligibility criteria (including diagnosis, socio-economic parameters, patient consent, agreement) to supply needed information. All this must be well-documented before starting the program.
4. Ensure you have proper control mechanisms to confirm eligibility criteria for all parties involved—the eligible patient population and, on the physician's side, which physician or group of physicians is eligible to take part in the program, including their roles and responsibilities; similarly, participating pharmacies and any TPC that may be involved, including their eligibil-

ity criteria and roles and responsibilities.
5. As described earlier, ensure you have proper control mechanisms to safeguard against misuse, abuse, or fraud.
6. Have a validated system to ensure data privacy and security. You should do this in cases where the company will have access to some patient data if allowed, and, obviously, it also applies to the third party who will be managing the program.
7. Ensure a proper pharmacovigilance program, as per company standards, and that the TPC, if involved, is well-aware of the pharmacovigilance requirements.
8. Have a documented exit strategy that provides clarity to all stakeholders, including the health authorities, about the impact of an exit, how it will be communicated to different stakeholders, and any action that should be taken if the program is terminated.
9. Train all relevant functions internally within the company, particularly the medical team, but also the TPC involved, and offer an abbreviated training program for participating physicians, pharmacies, and distributors to ensure the program runs efficiently.
10. Ensure periodic monitoring and a strong audit program. The monitoring program should be monthly, particularly at the beginning, to ensure that things run smoothly, and then less often if the program advances properly.

Alternative branding strategy (also known as access brand)

The second approach among the new access trends is the alternative branding strategy or access brand (AB). This is a new concept used by some MNCs in some of the MENA markets. Let's start with the definition of what an AB is.

Access brand or AB is when a company manufactures and commercializes a different brand of its primary commercially available brand name (e.g., the original brand). The AB has the same active ingredient and quality as the original brand, but at a significantly lower price; usually, it's less than or equal to 50 percent of the price of the original brand. The AB usually has the same dosage form as the original brand, but sometimes it has a different dosage form. For example, the original brand may be a prefilled syringe or an auto-injector, while the AB could be a lyophilized powder. Depending on the country's regulations, the market authorization holder (MAH) of the AB may be the same as the MAH of the original brand. In some countries, the law may not allow this, and the MAH of the AB must be a different legal entity.

In some cases, companies may choose to introduce the same AB (same name and packaging) in multiple countries that are interested in launching the AB. In other cases, the company may allow each country with a sizable market to introduce its own local AB. In cases where the AB is for multiple countries, the AB could be priced and commercialized in the COO (could be defined as the country where the product is made, the country where the MAH is registered, or the so-called batch-release country). If the company is planning to launch an AB, it needs to clearly understand the regulatory pathway and its requirements early on, before embarking on this strategy.

It's also important to note that, depending on the country's situation and the company's position, a company may introduce the AB as the only commercially available product on the market, or it may pursue the strategy of introducing both the original brand and the AB in the same country. This may occur where, for example, the company decides to launch the AB for the public sector, where prices are very low; therefore, the AB could be specifically serving the public channel, while the original brand will be mainly for the private market.

You may ask, why do companies introduce an AB? Why can't they commercialize the original brand? The answer is that most countries use the IRP system, explained in Chapter 3. Introducing the original brand means that the pricing of the product at a lower price in countries with affordability challenges (e.g., low-income countries) will not always be achievable. High-income countries will reference the low price of the original brand in low-income countries with affordability challenges, which means that these low-income countries would be used as a scapegoat, which is unfair. It is important to note here that in IRP countries, where the reference price is based on international non-proprietary names (INN), the AB strategy may not be a practical strategy to mitigate IRP (depending on MAH and other important factors). The other important consideration with AB is this: if the company decides to introduce the original brand in the low-price market at a significantly lower price, compared to the price in high-income countries, it creates parallel trade (also known as cross-border trade), which is undesirable. From a commercial perspective, it will be problematic, but from a pharmacovigilance perspective, it becomes a major challenge. Therefore, companies use the AB strategy as a potentially effective tool to expand access in countries where serious affordability challenges exist. Again, as said earlier, this concept of an AB strategy will work in some countries, but not in others.

Practical considerations when it comes to an access brand strategy

The first thing to consider is whether an AB is the right access strategy for the company and the intended market, given the different local considerations. The most important question that the company should ask itself is: Will an AB achieve the broad access desired? The answer to this question is important because the AB strategy, by definition, is to drive access deeper down the pyramid to reach patients who have serious affordability difficulties.

Second, will the introduction of the AB create price exposure risks to the original brand? If yes, then the company should not pursue this strategy and instead should consider any of the MEA schemes presented earlier.

Third, is the country's perception of the AB well established and favorable? This is an important point, and the company needs to consider the following questions:

- Does the health authority understand the value and why the company is introducing the AB?
- Is there a regulatory pathway for registering an AB?
- Do patients in the country understand and value the concept of an AB, and do they understand and trust the health-care system and the AB?

It's important to make sure that patients fully understand the access, fully embrace it, and are willing to use the AB, especially in countries where brand loyalty is prominent in the market.

The fourth point is whether the company's supply chain system is ready to manage the AB. This has two aspects: first, if the supply chain will be able to produce the AB for multiple markets; and second, if the company will localize the AB in individual markets (e.g., local manufacturing by the company or through a contract manufacturing organization). Therefore, the company needs to consider whether the costs and the margins from a financial P&L perspective are practical and sustainable over the long term. The company needs to make sure that the volume and the demand for the AB are large enough for the business case to be positive, compared to the original brand and employing different MEA schemes.

Looking into the future of the health-care environment

The lack of universal health insurance is what drives the need for patient affordability programs. Given the United Nations' mandate announced in September 2019 to drive the adoption of universal health insurance by 2030, the need for such programs will remain a key access initiative until that goal is achieved. The assumption then is that the OOP payments from patients will go toward the premium that will be set for expanded health coverage, and that there will be much less need for AB, as the direct negotiation between governments and companies will be around the pricing strategy of the original brand and leveraging the confidential net prices.

Summary

Addressing affordability for patients who pay for medicine out of pocket and patients who are under-insured is very important. PAPs should be designed carefully to ensure long-term integrity and sustainability. The AB strategy may be a suitable one to use in certain countries, where applicable and well accepted by all stakeholders. Until universal health insurance coverage is achieved, strategies to achieve sustainable access solutions using PAP or AB are essential components of expanding patient access to life-saving medicine that would otherwise be inaccessible to a large segment of the population. To achieve these broad access strategies, companies need to have the right MA team with the right capabilities, which is the topic of the next chapter.

7

THE WINNING MARKET ACCESS TEAM

What is the definition of a winning market access team?

The winning MA team is results-oriented and patient-centric in its approach to solving access problems. It focuses on what it needs to do well to win, and it makes use of the strengths of everyone on the expanded cross-functional team who are working on the product to deliver top results. It is the team empowered to make decisions on access and reimbursement. It is truly the team that practices the saying, *Where there's a will there's a way.*

In this chapter, we will cover the key aspects of the winning team—organizational setup, clear roles and responsibilities, core capabilities, and mindset. Let's start by talking about the organizational setup.

Organizational setup

In today's dynamic and challenging health-care environment, the success of many pharmaceutical companies depends on having a strong MA team responsible for all strategic and operational aspects of pricing, reimbursement, and MA. There are three critical aspects to cover before talking about the winning team itself.

1. The organization should be fully committed to the MA function. This means having a formal role profile for each level of the MA team that clearly describes the member's roles and responsibilities.
2. The organization should have a fully dedicated, properly staffed, well-funded team to do the programs and/or studies needed—whether it is real-world evidence, health economics and outcomes research (HEOR), or economic modeling—and make the decisions on access and reimbursement.
3. The organization should have the right reporting structure. It should view the MA function as a critical role, not as a support function, reporting directly to the company's president, and should be sitting on the leadership team of the company and/or the region.

The head of the MA function at the regional level should also have direct (solid line) or indirect (dotted line) reporting to the global MA team to give the voice of the EM on global access strategies. This gives more power to the function and allows it to have more resources.

Clear roles and responsibilities

It is important to have clear roles and responsibilities for each level of the MA team. This is to ensure that there is clarity within the whole organization on what the function is supposed to deliver. Ten different key activities define the roles the function should be focused on. While other activities fall within the remit of MA, these are the ones that I believe are important for emerging markets:

1. **Price management.** The MA function should manage all phases of pricing, from price vetting to price-setting and price netting, as described in Chapter 3.
2. **Early access to innovative therapy.** The MA team should lead the way by working cross-functionally, especially with the medical affairs team on any early access programs that the company has for products before registration and/or reimbursement.
3. **Economic modeling and real-world evidence generation.** The MA team should be directly responsible for all aspects of

RWE generation and communication to payer and formulary decision-makers. This includes all aspects of RWE, including economic data generation, economic modeling, budget impact models, and patient-reported outcomes (PRO) data. To the extent that the data generation involves medical data, the MA team should collaborate with the medical affairs team to ensure that data generated by the latter will also be maximized to fulfill MA needs.
4. **Design and implementation of MEA and PAP.** The MA team should drive the development and implementation of the right access solutions to fit different market archetypes. This involves collaborating with the cross-functional teams within the organization.
5. **Education and communication.** Specifically, the education of key decision-makers on the value proposition, whether it is clinical or economic, must ensure that the value is well understood before the price is communicated. The MA team should also develop and communicate key value messages (KVMs) to the right stakeholders. Where the KVMs are intended for a medical audience, the MA team should collaborate with the medical affairs team to ensure that these messages supporting the product's value proposition are communicated to the prescribers or the health-care providers.
6. **Advocacy.** The MA team should advocate sustainable solutions and shape the health-care environment to ensure that the policies and governance that are guiding the health-care delivery and practice in the country are conducive to a continuous stream of innovation and ensure that the latest trends in access solutions are well understood and, to the extent possible, implemented locally. It should do this in collaboration with the government affairs and policy/advocacy function in the company.
7. **Partnership.** The MA function should be the lead within the organization in developing long-term sustainable partnerships with the key stakeholders in the health-care system. As shown earlier, MA is a mindset, so the team leads the way but needs to collaborate on partnership initiatives, especially with medical

affairs, government affairs, and policy/advocacy teams.

8. **Monitoring.** Specifically, the MA team monitors the pricing and reimbursement environment in the country (or key accounts) to ensure they are up to date with what's going on in the health-care environment. Again, the team needs to collaborate with government affairs and policy/advocacy, where a function exists within the company, to also monitor any changes in the rules and regulations in the health-care environment in the country.

9. **Conduct advisory boards.** The MA team should conduct payer advisory boards to understand payer challenges and opportunities and to function as a sounding board for the company's approach to access and/or health-care challenges.

10. **Publication.** The MA team should lead the publication of key HEOR data that support the value proposition of the product based on evidence-based medicine principles and make sure that these publications are of high-quality, generated to support the value proposition, and communicated to key stakeholders.

Core capabilities

In addition to the organizational aspects needed, there are critical skill sets needed to build a winning MA team. These include the following skills:

1. **Technical capabilities.** Having the right technical capabilities, including HEOR. Although a lot of emerging market countries are not HTA markets, where formal health economic assessment is mandatory, many are moving in that direction. Therefore, having formal training in HEOR and/or HTA is highly desirable.

2. **Good understanding of pharmaceutical-pricing principles.** This is a critical aspect that the MA team should master, specifically because IRP is complicated. This means having knowledge of how the pricing principles work, the different aspects of pricing concerning access, and having a good understanding of tender management.

3. **Good commercial acumen.** This involves a good understanding of key aspects of the market and commercial operations and strategic marketing, in addition to a good understanding of key finance principles, especially with P&L financial analysis.
4. **Superior communication skills.** Communication is a critical aspect, both in terms of scientific communication when it comes to communicating HEOR data, as well as in terms of business communication when engaging with payers, either in negotiation or other commercial aspects.
5. **Relationship builder (e.g., advocacy).** The MA team should be skillful in building relationships across a broad spectrum of stakeholders, from payers to pay advisors, to clinicians, to P&T committee members, and patient groups.
6. **Solution-oriented and patient-centric.** The MA team should be patient-centric in designing and delivering access solutions. When cross-functional teams come up with proposals that may not be supportable, the team should offer practical ways to solve problems. Instead of saying, "You can't do it," the team should be able to say, "You can't do it this way, but here is how you can potentially do it."
7. **Ethical behavior.** This is to ensure that the business follows the highest ethical standards in a transparent and compliant way.
8. **Market shaping.** Good understanding of market-shaping and policy-shaping practices that shape the environment.

A mindset toward customer-centric value creation

As mentioned earlier, the goal of MA is to design and drive the implementation of customer-specific solutions to overcome access hurdles sustainably—that is, sustainable for the company, for the self-pay patient, and for the payer, whether private or public. In this regard, the team should strive for recognition as the partner of choice by the private and public sectors in the therapeutic areas that they focus on. While this is the goal of every company, the key differentiator is the company that can operationalize it. The company with the right MA mindset will be the one that will achieve recognition externally as a preferred partner of choice. To achieve this aim, the team must strive to understand each customer's operating business model to develop the right value-add solutions that address payer challenges while also optimizing patient outcomes. This means that they need to have the right customer-engagement approach. There are four vital steps in the customer value-creation framework that the MA function needs to focus on to deliver value-add solutions:

1. **Listen to the customer and analyze their needs.** The MA team should first and foremost listen to what the payer's interests, needs, and challenges are, understand where the pain points are, and the objectives of the stakeholders they are dealing with.
2. **Validate and prioritize.** After analyzing the insights gathered from the customer, the team should ensure that they understand what they have heard and can align it with the key priorities.
3. **Develop, design, and implement practical solutions that would deliver maximum value to their stakeholders.** This means proposing the right type of MEA or access solution, looking into the feasibility, practicality, and financials of both the company and the customer.
4. **Measurement.** After implementing the solutions to address the pain points, the focus should be on the questions: "What are the key metrics to measure that will communicate to the stakeholder the value of the program?" and "How can we use the learnings from the measurement to do continuous improvement, ensure sustainability, and deliver maximum value for the stakeholder?".

Now that we've talked about what we need to build a winning MA team from an organizational and operational perspective, let's talk about what **not** to do when building an MA function. First, do not promote people into the MA role just because they've been in the organization for a while. Unfortunately, many companies do exactly that. While this may make sense or sound intuitive, an employee who is very interested in MA does not necessarily have the capability needed to be successful. This is critical because giving people without proper qualifications a senior position just because they've been in the organization for a while means you are setting them up for failure.

Second, what we should also not do is to give the leader of regulatory affairs the MA role simply because they seem familiar with the pricing function. Regulatory affairs skill sets are very different from MA skill sets. While pricing is a part of both, most companies do not differentiate between price registration, which is part of the regulatory affairs function, and the bigger role of price management (vetting, setting, and netting), which is a core responsibility of MA.

Third, do not just delegate MA responsibility to the KAM team. Key account management is a critical function that is well-connected with MA, but it is a different function with a different skill set. This is probably one of the most common mistakes that organizations in emerging markets make when it comes to hiring people for the MA function. I know of cases where a successful KAM became a successful MA leader, which is fantastic. However, it should not be a given that a key account manager is ideal for the MA role. Similarly, organizations should not hire a sales team without strong access capability. To be successful in the MA function, they need to have the willingness to develop more skills and to have learning agility.

Lastly, some companies may resort to giving certain aspects of the MA function to medical affairs, especially in the era of cost containment where funding more staff may not be workable. While there is a close collaboration between the two functions, they are distinctly different functions. Sometimes, the line between data generation, particularly clinical economic data, can blur between MA and medical affairs. Data generation should be collaborative. Medical affairs will not be able to perform the function of MA. MA works well with medical affairs, but, again, it's a different function.

While "internal hiring" is an important concept that is a well-accepted practice in many companies, it should be done carefully and as part of a well-thought-out strategy to invest continuously in building the capability of employees. Equally important, though, is that the organization makes sure every function focuses on what it does best, to deliver what is expected of it and not do MA work—especially since many people in different functions are very drawn to MA and would like to "do the MA role."

Summary

Market access should be a truly organizational mindset. It's vital to have the function properly resourced in terms of the number of employees allocated to the function and the budget that is needed for the projects that the team conducts. Companies should fully invest in the function. They should continually build and improve the capabilities of the team through training, growth, and development opportunities. They should look for training programs that enhance the capabilities in each of the aspects that we've covered earlier, including negotiation, which we will cover in the next chapter. But, more importantly, the company should recognize MA by promoting good behavior and talent and recognizing these financially with rewards. It should also promote good MA talent into senior management roles within the organization. Lastly, having a winning MA team depends on hiring the people who can lead the function. The company needs to empower them to lead the function and make critical decisions, continue to invest in their capabilities, uplift their skill sets, and give them the organizational support needed in terms of staff and budget to perform their job well.

8

NEGOTIATIONS TO WIN ACCESS

Pharmaceutical innovations are a cornerstone of any health-care system in the world. Diffusion of pharmaceutical innovations in different countries will depend greatly on whether key stakeholders perceive their value. As discussed earlier, the perceived value will differ greatly from one stakeholder to another in different countries. Therefore, negotiations, especially with payers in the health-care system, to agree on value will be a key element in the timing and speed of diffusion of pharmaceutical innovations in emerging markets. In this chapter, we will focus on an important aspect of the MA role, which is negotiations, especially payer negotiations.

There are many different institutions and consultancy firms that conduct workshops, training, and mock negotiations. There are also many good books written on the subject. One that I've adapted to my daily practice and can highly recommend is a book titled *Getting to Yes: Negotiating Agreement without Giving In* by Roger Fisher and William Ury. The book is based on what it calls the seven critical elements of negotiations, which are relationships, communication, interests, options, legitimacy, commitment, and conclusion. The book explains each one of them in detail. I encourage every MA professional to read, understand, and practice the seven elements in their daily routine, or other similar books written on the subject. It will make them highly successful in payer negotiation.

This chapter, however, will focus on key practical aspects of payer negotiation skills needed for the MA team to be successful in their role. We will be talking about the following three aspects: first, principles to remember before, during, and after negotiations; second, the importance of practicing value-based negotiations; and third, the dos and don'ts in payer negotiations.

These are the key principles to remember before, during, and after negotiations:

1. It must be a win-win negotiation. Win-lose negotiations are short-lived.
2. "Put yourself in their shoes." What would you do if you were on the other side?
3. It's better to walk away sometimes rather than damage the relationship or lose the customer.
4. When you walk away, keep in touch with your stakeholders. Do not ignore them.
5. Always put it in writing; be very clear and specific.

In addition to the principles above, there are important aspects to watch out for in payer negotiations from both the humanistic and the business perspectives. From a humanistic perspective:

1. Relationships matter a lot everywhere, but they are far more important in the MENA region. Oftentimes, one person may hold the key to the whole market and oftentimes it's also a one-man show in many countries or key accounts. So, having a good relationship goes a long way.
2. Be extra careful not to alienate anyone. Even if they are not the main decision-maker now, you may cross paths with them again. The junior person today may be the decision-maker tomorrow. Make sure that you have good relationships with everybody and walk a fine line when you try to manage relationships.
3. Stand with people during their bad times; they will remember you in the good times.

4. In some countries, people change their jobs often—and the commitments they make will also change.
5. Be careful with written communications. People share everything, especially in these times, using social media like WhatsApp, Facebook, or Twitter. Assume that every piece of information you share will be shared widely.

On the business side, it's important to keep in mind the following key aspects:

1. *Beware abrupt decisions.* Unfortunately, many countries make decisions too abruptly and implement them too quickly. As a result, new rules sometimes become effective at once or within a couple of months, which can have a significant impact on business.
2. *Be careful with multi-year contracts.* Contracts, especially multi-year ones, are usually binding. But sometimes, people try to renegotiate midway through the contract, especially in cases where the customer knows the company will do everything it can to preserve the relationship. Therefore, be careful with multi-year contracts and how they can potentially change midway.
3. *Take care when going into contracts.* Because of the way governmental systems and business relationships work in the region, it is not customary for companies to challenge governments on certain aspects (or challenge them in court). Therefore, be very careful when going into contracts, especially enforceability terms and how you would implement the contract without creating friction with government or semi-governmental institutions.
4. *Do your homework.* In our line of business, forecasting makes a lot of sense. But often, it's not done, or not done well, which means that it can add to market volatility. Therefore, when going into payer negotiations, especially on volume-based agreements, make sure you do your homework and prepare scenarios beyond what the payer asked for—this will help avoid future problems.

5. *Agility is a must-have—not a nice to have—in the MENA environment.* Because of the volatile nature of the region, agility is very important. You need to be able to act quickly, decisively, and avoid long bureaucratic processes.

Value-based negotiations

When it comes to value-based negotiations, it's important to promote a sustainable health-care system and use the value-based framework. This means that the MA function should always advocate and promote the principles of a sustainable health-care system before negotiations, during negotiations, and after negotiations. It should emphasize three things—predictability, transparency, and sustainability. Sustainability is particularly important. The six principles of a sustainable health-care system that a value-based negotiation should advocate are:

1. **Focus on health, not just health-care**—meaning, it's important to promote disease prevention, not just the treatment.
2. **Focus on value-based health-care, not volume-based health-care**. A negotiation should always advocate promoting interventions that add value to the system, not the volume of medicines sold.
3. **Focus on quality of care, not quantity of care**. Quality should always be at the center of health-care delivery, especially nowadays when payers everywhere use quality metrics, performance indicators, and scorecards.
4. **Focus on population health indicators and KPIs, not market share data**. Emphasize the impact of VBC on important global population metrics and do not just focus on market share data.
5. **Focus on patient empowerment, not just patient count**. Patient-centricity should be the principle in all activities of MA and cross-functional teams.
6. **Promote prescribing what patients need, not what is profitable**. This is the best way for you to ensure that health-care resources are well-spent and that there will be a continuous flow of innovations to the health-care system.

Next, let's focus on the **dos and don'ts** in payer negotiations.

Dos and don'ts in payer negotiations

Do ...

- be ready, know the situation, and gather as much data as possible.
- ask customers what they want to achieve and why before you negotiate.
- prepare different scenarios ahead of time.
- go to the payer in good times, not just in bad times.
- repeat what you heard and confirm your understanding before you reply to queries.
- leave a positive impression with your customer so they welcome you the next time.

Don't ...

- assume what people say publicly will translate into what they do in practice.
- start a price war! It can spiral downward rapidly and destroy the market.
- volunteer more services once the customer agrees to your offer.
- assume that people understand what you mean. State your position clearly and ask: "Is it clear to everyone?".
- be intimidated, but be respectful and firm in your position.
- make a commitment you cannot keep.
- compromise your ethics to please your boss. Your reputation will always follow you.

Summary

Winning in negotiation is about winning the customer for the long run, not just the immediate deal. Value should always be at the center of the negotiation. Your win is as good as your negotiation skills. So be extremely well prepared before you walk into any negotiation. Lastly, never damage your reputation when negotiating—your reputation will always follow you.

CONCLUSION
THREE TAKEAWAYS

Now that we have covered the key pillars of how to win market access in an emerging market, I will summarize the three takeaways from the book:

1. **Mindset is everything** individually and organizationally. Developing a customized solution to overcome access challenges will vary by country, therapeutic area, and payer type. This requires a cross-functional team approach to develop and implement ethical, compliant, and sustainable solutions.
2. **Organizational commitment** to market access, starting with a proper setup of the MA function to funding and empowerment, is critical. Without that, the organization will not be able to harness the full potential of the lifesaving innovations they bring to markets.
3. **Operational excellence** is a must. MA leaders in the organization must have the knowledge and know-how to navigate the tough issues that market access continuously faces, within the organization and externally with payers and reimbursement authorities. The personal commitment of MA leaders to continue to learn and grow, leveraging on the strength of the different

teams within the organization, and purposeful engagement with external stakeholders in the health-care ecosystem will determine true success in market access.

The purpose of this book is to help professionals in the field get a better, deeper, and more practical understanding of the key pillars of market access in emerging markets. The true benefit that you will get out of this book will depend on how you translate the learning to action by driving the implementation of the concepts presented in the book. I started the book with the saying *Where there's a will there's a way*; if you believe in this saying, after reading the book, I hope you will be motivated to apply another saying: *It's not about ideas. It's about making ideas happen.*

For further discussion on the book or questions, refer to "Author Contact" and follow the instructions.

ABOUT THE AUTHOR

After graduating from the College of Pharmacy, University of Illinois at Chicago, and completing my Pharmacy Practice Residency, I joined the pharmaceutical industry back in 1996, way before the market access function even existed. Back then, the focus was on "pharmacoeconomics" and "outcomes research." Over the past 24 years working in the top 10 pharmaceutical companies, I established Market Access, Health Economics and Outcomes Research functions, and led the development and implementation of market access strategies for many high-value innovative products in developed and emerging markets. In this book, I am sharing the extensive experience I gained over the years, as part of my endeavor to help future leaders in this field, and more importantly, to improve access to innovative medicine in emerging markets.

—Dr. Kasem Akhras

www.ingramcontent.com/pod-product-compliance
Lightning Source LLC
Chambersburg PA
CBHW021443080526
44588CB00009B/665